Governing Britain

MANCHESTER
1824

Manchester University Press

Governing Britain

Parliament, ministers and our ambiguous constitution

Philip Norton

Manchester University Press

Published by Manchester University Press
Altrincham Street, Manchester M1 7JA
www.manchesteruniversitypress.co.uk

British Library Cataloguing-in-Publication Data
A catalogue record for this book is available from the British Library

ISBN 978 1 5261 4545 1 hardback

First published 2020

Typeset by Newgen Publishing UK
Printed in Great Britain
by TJ International Ltd, Padstow

Contents

Tables

Preface

Constitutions, as John Stuart Mill observed in 1861, did not emerge one morning fully formed.[1] The British constitution in particular has developed over centuries, indeed a millennium. Its history and form give rise to ambiguities and uncertainties. Michael Foley, in *The Silence of Constitutions*, identified constitutional 'abeyances', understandings that are largely unspoken and which may embody contradictions and uncertain edges, and which are maintained by 'studied inattention'.[2] Abeyances, he noted, are valuable, not in spite of their obscurity, but because of it.

In recent years, conflicts within British politics and major constitutional reforms, notable for their number as well as significance, have given rise to previously unspoken understandings being questioned. 'Studied inattention' has meant that there is little history of debating the constitution as a constitution.[3] Previous changes, even when of major constitutional import, have generally occurred on a discrete basis and been adapted to the nation's constitutional architecture before further change has occurred.[4] However, when change has taken place on a substantial scale, with several major reforms occurring within a short period of time, there has been uncertainty in knowing the implications for the nation's constitution. When the 'English question', discussed later in this volume, became an issue in UK politics, a Commons select committee noted that not only was there no consensus about the answer to the question, but that there was no agreement as to the question.[5]

The purpose of this work is neither to provide a comprehensive introduction to the constitution of the United Kingdom, nor offer prescriptions for change. There are various works that already do one or both. Rather, it draws out questions thrown up by the changes of recent years. They are questions that in some measure break the silence of the constitution. They are elucidated through examining the principles underpinning the constitution, primarily parliamentary sovereignty and the rule of law, constitutional conventions and practices, the extent to which they are contested and how they shape the relationships at the heart of government. The focus is on features that are ambiguous or misunderstood and the implications of recent constitutional and political change.

It is important to note that this is not a work of constitutional theory. Although it draws on some theory to explain relationships, it is not designed to provide a theory that explains the nature of the constitution. Insofar as there is an explanatory framework, it is to be found in the nature of problem solving. Sartori identified two approaches: the rational and the empirical.[6] The rational is concerned with abstraction, emphasising the need for deductive consistency. The empirical is concerned with what is and what can be seen and touched, rejecting dogma and abstract reasoning in favour of experience. The United States adopts the former approach and the United Kingdom the latter. The difference is well encapsulated in Vivien Hart's observation that 'In America the emphasis has been on what democracy is and *should* be, while Britain has been characterised by a more pragmatic and less urgent emphasis on what democracy is and *can* be'.[7] This has informed each nation's approach to the rest of the world as well as its own constitution.[8] The British approach, as may be inferred from the following chapters, has the advantage of some flexibility, but at the expense of a codified set of rules. When several changes take place at the same time, there is the challenge of making sense of how each impacts on the constitution as well as understanding how the constitution itself holds together.

The inspiration for this work is a short monograph penned initially in the 1950s by Geoffrey Marshall and Graeme Moodie, *Some Problems of the Constitution*. It identified several problems and offered short discussions of each. We follow the same pattern. The chapters are designed to be accessible and each written in order to be reasonably self-contained, enabling readers to skip and dip as desired. As with *Some Problems of the Constitution*, the work is written for the student and anyone with an interest in the constitution. In writing it, I have benefited greatly from discussion with fellow parliamentarians and academic colleagues who toil in the disciplines of politics, law and history, as well as from the comments of the publisher's anonymous reviewers. Any errors or omissions are my responsibility alone. I welcome comments from readers, not least if they spot any errors.

Philip Norton
January 2020

Notes

1 Mill 1968: 177.
2 Foley 1989: 9.
3 Norton 2011a: 12.
4 Stevens 2002: xiii.
5 Justice Committee, House of Commons 2009: 50–69.
6 See Dahl 1966: 353.
7 Hart 1978: 202–3.
8 Norton 2010: 28–9.

Chapter 1

Britain's uncodified constitution

A constitution is the body of laws, rules and customs that establishes the organs of a state (executive, legislature, judiciary), how those organs relate to one another, and the relations between those organs and the citizen. Most, but not all, nations embody the key provisions in a single codified document. There is thus a document with the designation of 'the constitution'. However, the provisions extend beyond the document to encompass judicial decisions (interpreting the words of the document), laws that supplement the document, as well as rules of behaviour that are not legally enforceable, but which are complied with invariably (conventions) or usually, though not invariably (practice). The US constitution – a short document compared to some constitutions – vests judicial power 'in one supreme Court, and in such inferior Courts as the Congress may from time to time ordain and establish' (Article III(1)). Judicial power is not defined. The power to interpret the constitution and strike down measures as unconstitutional (judicial review) was read into the constitution by the supreme court in *Marbury* v. *Madison* in 1803. The size of the supreme court is determined by statute, as is the appellate jurisdiction of the court. It was a convention that the president serve no more than two terms. President Franklin Roosevelt broke the convention in 1940 by standing for a third term. The two-term limit

1

would thus have acquired the status of a practice had the document not been amended, so the limit is now formally enshrined (22nd amendment).

The definition is important for explaining the nature of the constitution of the United Kingdom. It is distinctive for the form it takes, in that it is uncodified. There is no one document drawing the basic provisions together. Rather, there is a body of laws (statutes and common law), conventions and practices that have developed over time, existing within, and deriving from, a view of the form of government most appropriate to the nation.

The UK is thus distinctive, one of only three nations that does not have a codified constitution. However, it is not so distinctive in another respect that is fundamental to understanding constitutions. That is, the extent to which their provisions are accepted and upheld.[1] In some nations, constitutions derive their legitimacy from popular acceptance that they are superior bodies of law by which all are bound, whatever their status. Here, the ruling regime is subordinate to the constitution. There is thus a culture that can be described as one of constitutionalism. In other nations, there are constitutions, but no constitutionalism. Here, the constitution is subordinate to the regime, to be used or ignored as the rulers dictate. Constitutions are not so much formulated and agreed through a process recognised by the population as legitimate, but rather imposed from above, possibly endorsed by plebiscite, but in conditions where citizens feel they have no real choice.

There are also gradations in terms of constraints accepted within those nations where constitutionalism exists. Barber has argued that it extends beyond seeing it purely as a constraint on authority (negative constitutionalism) to advancing certain principles for the benefit of society (positive constitutionalism).[2] One finds constitutionalism primarily in liberal-democracies, where supremacy of the general will is balanced by acceptance of liberal values.[3] LeDuc *et al.* found that some nations were electoral autocracies, holding elections, but not ones that were free or fair.[4] Some nations were electoral democracies, where free elections were held, but with little or no protection for minorities or individuals: in effect, democracies rather than liberal-democracies. Others were liberal democracies, ensuring a balance between majority rule and the rights of minorities and individuals. In some nations, there may be deemed to be a weak culture of constitutionalism, whereas in liberal-democracies one finds the strongest form.

The United Kingdom is not alone in having a culture of constitutionalism. It is a feature of western nations. However, it may be argued that the strength of that culture has made possible the endurance of an uncodified constitution. Some of the basic rules in a society may be so well established that it is not necessary to enshrine them formally. Where the rules are not well ingrained in citizens' consciousness, there may be a need to embody them in a codified constitution.[5] Constitutionalism in the UK has developed over a substantial period, unencumbered in recent centuries by regime change and the necessity to start afresh. That culture has underpinned a constitution that, in its form and acceptance, has been widely admired. However, what we have witnessed in recent years has been a tension that has put strains on the constitution, both in its form and its acceptance. There have been changes to the constitution, demands for more, and calls for a new constitution, both in purpose and form.

A constitution taking shape

The constitution has taken shape over centuries, the basis of the existing constitution being confirmed in 1688. Prior to then, the form and acceptance of the constitution had evolved. One can see its origins in the coronation oath of the tenth century, which included the words 'that I forbid all rapine and injustice to men of all conditions'. The coronation charter of Henry I of 1100 promised to take away all 'bad customs' by which the kingdom had been unjustly oppressed. The charter of 1215 (variously reissued in different and modified forms and later known as *Magna Carta*), by which leading barons sought to curtail the powers of King John, has since acquired totemic status. It has been portrayed as the origin of certain basic rights, such as jury trials and *habeas corpus*, but which in practice has been more important for symbolism than substance.[6] (Both jury trials and *habeas corpus* developed later and unrelated to the charter.) A parliament evolved in the thirteenth century and over two centuries acquired functions that remain its principal tasks: debating the demands of the crown for legislation or supply before assenting to them, scrutinising the conduct of the administration, and raising and seeking a redress of grievances. Parliament and king variously clashed, with the crown being limited because of a conflict that was bloody – the English civil war, resulting in the king, Charles I, being executed in 1649 – and one that wasn't, the 'glorious revolution' of 1688–9, when James II fled and was deemed to have abdicated.

The period of republican rule (1649–60) was notable for producing two written constitutions – the Instrument of Government of 1653,[7] followed by the Humble Petition and Advice 1657 – but with the Restoration of 1660 seeing a deliberate reversion to what had existed before 1649. The codified constitutions were short-lived and the absence of seismic historical conflicts since has denied the conditions usually deemed necessary for crafting a new constitution. The glorious revolution established, through the Bill of Rights 1689, the basic relationship between crown and Parliament – that the king could not legislate without the assent of Parliament – and confirmed what has been characterised as the cornerstone of the constitution: the doctrine of parliamentary sovereignty. Parliamentary sovereignty was already part of the constitution, though some jurists had previously contested it. Now it was beyond challenge. As Dicey was later to define it (see Chapter 2), it meant that the outputs of Parliament could be set aside by nobody other than Parliament itself and that no Parliament could bind its successor.

Subsequent centuries saw changes, but within the basic framework established in 1689. Industrialisation and a growing population led to demands in the nineteenth century to widen the franchise, resulting in Reform Acts that ensured that by the end of the century the majority of working men had the vote. The outputs of Parliament may be binding (parliamentary sovereignty) but Dicey recognised that they were likely to be shaped by popular input (popular sovereignty). As he noted, 'the will of the electors shall by regular and constitutional means always in the end assert itself as the predominant influence in the country. But this is a political, not a legal fact'.[8] Parliament provided the constitutional means for giving effect to the will. The result was to establish the House of Commons as the body as the heart of the British political system.[9] Whoever could gain a majority in the House of Commons could determine the outcome of public policy.

The result was the emergence of an eponymous form of government – the Westminster parliamentary system. Organised mass-membership political parties developed as a result of a mass franchise and fought under the first-past-the-post electoral system for the spoils of electoral victory. The system facilitated, though did not guarantee, two-party conflict, with one side becoming the government and the other forming an official opposition. (The concept of 'Her Majesty's opposition' is very much a characteristic of Westminster parliaments.)[10] There was a structured adversarial relationship between the two. It epitomised what Anthony King termed the opposition mode of executive-legislative relations. The two parties, he wrote, have no incentive to agree: 'their aim is not accommodation but conquest'.[11] The chamber of the House of Commons is the arena for the contest between the two. The conflict may be sharp, but with both sides accepting the rules within which they operate. The relationship has been characterised by an equilibrium of legitimacy,[12] opposition parties recognising that the government is entitled to get its business, but the government accepting that the opposition is entitled to be heard. Each is constrained by the realisation that at the next election they may change places.

The model also stipulates the relationship of Parliament to the people.[13] At the heart of the relationship is the concept of accountability. Government is chosen through elections to the House of Commons and that government is then accountable for its actions to the people at the next election and, between elections, to the people's representatives in the House of Commons. There is one body – the party in government – that is responsible for public policy. The principle of collective responsibility ensures that government faces Parliament, and electors, as a united entity and relies for its continuation in office on the confidence of the House of Commons. There is a clear line of accountability to the House and to the electors.

By the twentieth century, the UK had a constitution that was both stable and well regarded. The constitutionalism that had developed over time, indeed over a millennium, was well ingrained. Conflict within the kingdom had essentially been over the need for the constitution to constrain authority. There was now perceived to be a commendable constraint, the crown constrained by a popularly elected House of Commons, elected by the people, and with Parliament itself recognising the imperatives of respecting liberty and the rule of law.

The constitution rested on popular acceptance, embodying the nineteenth-century belief in balance, a belief shared by liberals such as John Stuart Mill and conservatives such as the 3rd Marquess of Salisbury.[14] It balanced Old Tory and modified Whig beliefs in the emphasis accorded government and Parliament respectively. Government was dependent on other organs of the state to achieve its policies and recognised the limits of the state.[15] It 'balanced the need to achieve the consent of the people and the need to govern, working within an established order, one recognised and accepted by both governed and governors, the electors and the elected'.[16]

The system of government was extolled on grounds of account-ability, effectiveness, responsiveness and flexibility.[17] Government was accountable and could be turned out at the next election. Election day was, in Karl Popper's words, 'judgment day'. After being elected on a programme, government usually enjoyed a par-liamentary majority to deliver it. Governments in post-war years had a good record of implementing manifesto promises,[18] any high-profile failures being exploited by its opponents. Although able to deliver a coherent programme of public policy, governments nonetheless kept an eye on the popular mood in between elections, both in the country and in the House of Commons. If they ran into trouble, they could adapt. Insofar as flexibility is a desirable feature of a constitution, 'it is a function which the doctrine of parliamentary sovereignty could be understood to fulfil in the UK'.[19] The system made possible such adaptation, not only in response to popular pressure, but also in dealing with emergencies. Government could legislate quickly, or utilise prerogative powers, if the necessity arose, as with the commitment of forces abroad. In 1982, for example, the government moved rapidly, not least under pressure from the House of Commons, to despatch a task force to the Falkland Islands, a British overseas territory, after they were invaded by Argentinian troops.

This combination of attributes was seen as rendering the Westminster model both distinctive and preferable to other systems, which could not match it. The system of government also enjoyed political support. The Conservatives extolled the balance between effectiveness and consent.[20] The Labour Party saw winning a majority in the House of Commons as the means to fulfilling a radical social policy and as a result was constitutionally conservative.[21] Liberals saw it as a limited system, with the rights of the individual protected and, indeed, expanding through exten-sion of the franchise and economic reforms.[22] Politics thus take place within an accepted constitutional framework. The constitu-tion itself was not a matter of political dispute. Discussion of the constitution was viewed primarily as a matter for lawyers rather than political scientists.

The constitution under pressure

All this was to change in the latter half of the twentieth century, and especially in the final decades of the century. The constitution has moved from being largely settled to being contested. We can identify three overlapping stages. There were demands for discrete changes to the constitution, advocacy of different approaches to constitutional change, mostly favouring a new constitutional settlement, and calls for a codified constitution.

Demands for discrete changes. The period from the 1960s onwards was notable for demands for constitutional reforms. The nation faced relative economic decline. There were political problems, not least deriving from 'the troubles' in Northern Ireland, when troops had to be sent to try to maintain order, and attempts by successive governments to reform industrial relations, leading to conflict with trade unions. There were growing nationalist movements in Scotland and Wales, especially the former, calling for more autonomy or independence. There were two general elections in one year (1974), neither producing a government with a clear working majority.

Calls for reform of the electoral system began to be heard, with some commentators arguing that the present system was unfair and not delivering what had previously been claimed for it. According to S. E. Finer, the adversarial conflict between the parties – a new party coming into office and reversing the policies of its predecessors – militated against the continuity needed for economic development.[23] Others focused on the capacity of governments returned on a minority of votes – the last government to be returned with more than 50 per cent of the votes cast was in 1935 – to mobilise a parliamentary majority to pass laws that impinged on the rights of the individual. In 1976, former cabinet minister Lord Hailsham warned of the dangers of what he termed an elective dictatorship,[24] with power concentrated increasingly in cabinet and prime minister. What had changed was not so much the actual powers, but rather their use or perception of how they could be used. The answer for some, like Hailsham – though he later recanted after again becoming a cabinet minister – was to introduce a bill of rights to constrain an over-mighty government. There were also calls to devolve powers from the centre to elected bodies in Scotland and Wales. A Royal Commission on the Constitution, which reported in 1973, advocated some measure of devolution.

Some reforms were implemented in this period. The most important in the 1970s was the UK's membership of the European Communities (EC), taking effect on 1 January 1973, having been pursued by successive governments for economic and political reasons. It created constitutional challenges, not being wholly compatible with extant constitutional norms, and introduced a new juridical dimension to the constitution. Senior courts could now strike down provisions of UK law as incompatible with EC law. For the first time, referendums were held at other than local government level. Parliament legislated for a referendum in Northern Ireland on the issue of the province's constitutional status and for a UK-wide referendum in 1975 on continued membership of the EC. For the UK, a national referendum was a novel constitutional departure. The Labour government of 1974–9 also sought to introduce devolution for Scotland and Wales, but the outcomes of referendums in both failed to meet the threshold stipulated by Parliament.

More constitutional reforms followed under the Labour government returned in 1997. It achieved devolution in Scotland, Wales and Northern Ireland, with powers being devolved to elected bodies in each. It achieved enactment of the Human Rights Act 1998, enshrining most provisions of the European Convention on Human Right into UK law and adding to the juridical dimension of the constitution. It also achieved reform of the House of Lords, removing most hereditary peers from membership, and passage of the Constitutional Reform Act 2005, creating a supreme court for the United Kingdom in place of the appellate committee of the House of Lords. Other reforms included enactment of a Freedom of Information Act and the Constitutional Reform and Governance Act 2010 which, among things, put the civil service on a statutory basis.

Constitutional reform was not stilled with Labour losing office in 2010. The coalition government of 2010–15 achieved passage of the Fixed-Term Parliaments Act 2011, providing for a fixed-term of five years other than in specified circumstances, and an act providing for a UK-wide referendum on a change of the electoral system for parliamentary elections. (By two-to-one, voters rejected the introduction of the alternative vote.) It also acquiesced in a referendum in Scotland in 2014 on the issue of independence. There was a decentralisation of power to some regional and local government in England, especially urban areas in the north. The Conservative government returned in 2015 legislated for a referendum on whether the UK should stay in or leave the European Union. In 2016, the result was 52 per cent to 48 per cent in favour of leave. The government then set about legislating for withdrawal from the EU (Brexit), but ran into significant problems in mobilising parliamentary support for achieving that outcome. The fallout from the referendum included the resignation of two prime ministers (David Cameron in 2016, Theresa May in 2019), two early general elections (2017, 2019), an attempt by MPs to wrest control of public policy from ministers, and the biggest defeat in the House of Commons ever suffered by a government.

There are two generalisations to be made about these changes. First, they were significant for their extent and the pace of imple- mentation.[25] As Robert Stevens observed in *The English Judges*, the nation moved from change on a glacial scale to one unseen since the late seventeenth and early eighteenth centuries.[26] Second, the changes were essentially disparate and discrete. They lacked any intellectual coherence. Some were the product of principle, others of political expediency. All three UK-wide referendums, as well as those in Scotland and Wales in the 1970s, could be seen to derive from political imperatives. There was no overarching view of the constitution driving change.

Demands for a new constitutional settlement. The failure to pursue an overarching approach was not because no such approach was articulated. Towards the end of the twentieth century, various intellectually coherent approaches to constitutional change began to take shape, putting the case for a new constitutional settlement. They sought in differing degrees to modify or replace the existing constitution with one based on specified defining principles. The demands for a new constitution did not go unchallenged.

At least seven approaches to constitutional change were discernible: high Tory, group, socialist, Marxist, new right, liberal and traditional (or Westminster model).[27] The high Tory approach lauded the constitution as being evolutionary, but in practice, adopted a stance that was static; it saw the existing constitution as sound and not in need of any change. The end-result was thus what exists now. For the rest, there were future goals. The group, or corporatist, approach favoured decision-making by consensus among different groups in society; government was not autonomous, but a partner. In its pure form, it favoured corporatism. The socialist approach wanted decision-making determined from the bottom-up, with intra-party democracy at the heart of the system, and obstacles to achieving a socialist programme – such as the European Union and the House of Lords – swept away. The Marxist approach envisaged a collapse of the existing system through the weight of its own contradictions, to be replaced by a people's democracy. The new right approach favoured a constitution that embraced the principle of the market.

Debate, however, tended to focus on the liberal approach, favouring a fragmentation of power, and the traditional approach, adhering to the Westminster model of government. The liberal approach was premised on power becoming too centralised, with inadequate protection for the individual and minorities. The centralised state needed to be replaced by one where power was distributed among different bodies, not dissimilar to continental federal nations. Adherents to this approach advocated an entrenched bill of rights, more devolution (the pure form of the approach favours federalism), an elected second chamber, elections to the first chamber based on a system of proportional representation, all to be embodied in, and protected by, a codified constitution. The traditional, or Westminster, approach countered by making the case for the attributes of the existing system. Unlike the high Tory approach, it accepted change, but change to strengthen rather than destroy the existing system.

The case for the liberal approach was put by reform organisations, notably Charter '88, founded on the tercentenary of the glorious revolution to argue for a new constitutional settlement. Not surprisingly, it was also advanced by the Liberal Democrat Party. Some bodies, such as the Institute for Public Policy Research (IPPR), published what amounted to draft constitutions. The approach was countered by Conservative, and some Labour, politicians who argued for the existing Westminster model. Prime minister John Major (1990–7) was to the fore in thinking about and articulating the case for the existing constitution.[28] There was thus a debate about the nation's constitutional future, derived from clear principles, but it was detached from the political reality of changes that were made to the nation's constitutional fabric.

Calls for a codified constitution. Calls for a codified constitution have become more prominent in recent years.[29] They have gained currency because of tensions in the union of the United Kingdom – especially in Scotland and Northern Ireland – and Brexit.[30] The latter may have exacerbated the former in that a majority in Scotland and in Northern Ireland voted for the UK to remain in the EU, whereas a majority in England and Wales voted to leave. The tensions appear to underpin a growing dissatisfaction with the system of government. The 2019 Hansard Society *Audit of Political Engagement* found that 72 per cent of those surveyed felt that the system of governing needs 'quite a lot' or 'a great deal' of improvement, the highest level it had been in the Audit series.[31]

Brexit has been advanced by some as the tipping point making the case for a codified constitution. The effect of conflict, according to Vernon Bogdanor, 'is to inject further uncertainty as to what the British constitution actually is, uncertainty that can only be resolved by a codified British constitution'.[32] The UK, he argues, will move from a protected system, the treaties of the EU being akin to a codified constitution, to an unprotected one.[33] A UK codified constitution would, it is argued, provide protection.

The case is disputed in terms of demand, merit and achievability. In terms of demand, Jeff King has argued that opinion polls show people are opposed to the status quo. 'Opinion polling consistently shows that people want a reformed House of Lords, a different voting system, and a written constitution.'[34] When offered a (leading) question on whether 'Britain needs a written constitution providing clear legal rules within which government ministers and civil servants are forced to operate',[35] 74 per cent agreed.

The case against is that the claim of public support falls foul of the very problem King identifies with referendums in that they offer a 'take it or leave it', or binary, choice, the very type of choice offered in questions utilised to make the case for a codified constitution. Wording also matters. Injecting justifications can produce respondents giving mutually exclusive answers. (One poll found 72 per cent of respondents wanted at least half the members of the House of Lords to be elected and 75 per cent wanted to retain a mainly appointed House.)[36] Furthermore, the question does not address the extent to which electors accord it priority. Some commentators have argued that there is no obvious public demand for a codified constitution.[37] Support for change may be broad, but it is not deep.

For proponents, a codified constitution offers clarity and protection. People would know the key provisions. Those provisions, assuming an entrenched document (that is, amendable by some extraordinary process), would be safe from being the plaything of government. It would not be able to be changed simply by a transient majority in the two Houses of Parliament. For traditionalists, it challenges some of the key attributes of the Westminster model, not least effectiveness and flexibility. Government and Parliament would be operating in what may at times be a constitutional straitjacket. It challenges fundamentally acceptance of political sovereignty as the will of the majority, albeit tempered by Parliament. To opponents, it would transfer power from an elected body (Parliament) to the courts, with judges determining the meaning of its provisions.

Insofar as the aim is to create legal rules to limit ministers and civil servants in how they operate, it is not clear why a codified constitution is preferable to an act of Parliament to achieve that outcome. Likewise, with holding together the different parts of the Union. One body, the constitutional reform group, has made the case for an Act of Union Bill, underpinning the union and governing the relationship between its different parts. Brice Dickson has advocated a Constitutional Reform Act, covering rights as well as the purpose of the United Kingdom.[38]

Although advocated as a response to constitutional conflicts of recent years, it is unclear as to how a codified constitution would be a solution to those conflicts. Some of the problems encountered, as over the use of the prerogative to prorogue Parliament, have been encountered in other nations. Absent perfect knowledge as to its content, which no one has, one cannot know the effects of a new constitution. One would also have the same conundrum as with any codified constitution. Citizens would know what it says, but not necessarily know what it means until those vested with its interpretation, usually the courts, have interpreted authoritatively its provisions. A 'written' constitution, as we have noted, is more than the document.

Conclusion

The British constitution has moved from being settled, exhibiting what Brazier has termed 'the triumph of gradualism',[39] to being unsettled and, indeed, uncertain. It has witnessed change on a scale unprecedented in modern British history, change that has been pursued in constitutional silos, each reform taking place largely independently of the others, and with more reforms being advanced and disparate demands for a new constitutional settlement, both in substance and form, forming part of political debate.

The nature of debate about the constitution reflects an inherent conundrum. There are calls for a new constitution, in one form or another. They derive from dissatisfaction with current framework. However, a new constitution requires popular agreement for its content and form. The debate derives from an absence of agreement. Some politicians have advocated a constitutional convention, composed of members of the public and/or experts, to debate and draw up a new constitution. The focus is on identifying a replacement for what presently exists. This rests on reaching agreement on a convention and, more especially, its outputs.[40] The problem, according to Anthony King, is that it is more likely to divide than unite.[41] As the debate in 2019 on Brexit revealed, it is difficult to reach agreement where people adopt mutually exclusive positions, with neither being willing to engage with the other. Commitment to constitutional processes is subordinated to achieving a political goal: 'I am against referendums except on x', with x being the favoured political goal that has proved unachievable through the existing political process.

The constitution is thus contested, but the way forward is unclear and uncertain. It has changed on a substantial scale, but the basics of the Westminster model of government remain in place. For supporters of the traditional approach, change has gone too far. For supporters of the liberal and some other approaches, it has not gone far enough.

Notes

1   See Norton 2012a: 72–3.
2   Barber 2018.
3   See Sunstein 2001.
4   LeDuc *et al.* 2010: 12.
5   See Hayek 1979: 108; Castiglione 1996: 8–9.
6   Sumption 2015; Norton 2016a.
7   Heath 1967: 15–34.
8   Dicey 1959: 73.
9   Keir 1966: 463; Norton 1981: ch. 2.
10 See Kaiser 2008: 21.
11 King 1976: 18.
12 Norton 2001: 28.
13 Norton 2019a: 999–1000.
14 Norton 1982: 23; see also Amery 1953: 15.
15 Norton 1981: 276, 280.
16 Norton 2012b: 129.
17 Norton 2012b: 128–9.
18 Rose 1984: 64–7; Hofferbert and Budge 1992: 151–82.
19 Gordon 2015: 22.
20 Norton 2012b: 121–32; Amery 1953: 15–17.
21 Dorey 2008.
22 Birch 1964: ch. 4; Norton 1982: 276.
23 Finer 1975.
24 Hailsham, 1976.
25 Finn and Seldon 2013: 18–19.
26 Stevens 2002: xiii.
27 Norton 2010: 434–7.
28 Norton 2017a.
29 See e.g. Brazier 2008: ch. 11; Blick 2015.
30 Bogdanor 2019.
31 Hansard Society 2019: 8.

32 Bogdanor 2019: 261.
33 Bogdanor 2019: 273–4.
34 King 2019: 6.
35 Cited by King 2019: 6, n13.
36 Norton 2017b: 67–8.
37 See Dickson 2019: 36–7.
38 Dickson 2019: 101–2.
39 Brazier 2008: 15.
40 Leyland 2016: 305.
41 King 2007: 363.

Chapter 2

Constitutional twin pillars: does parliamentary sovereignty trump the rule of law?

In his classic work, *Introduction to the Law of the Constitution*, first published in 1885, A. V. Dicey argued that 'at all times since the Norman Conquest' two features had characterised the political institutions of England. One was the undoubted supremacy of central government, with royal supremacy having passed into the sovereignty of Parliament. 'The second of these features', he wrote, 'which is closely connected with the first, is the rule or supremacy of law'.[1] For Dicey, they were the twin pillars of the constitution. They remain core tenets of the UK constitution.

Dicey's definition of parliamentary sovereignty has entered the lexicon of constitutional law:

> The principle of Parliamentary sovereignty means neither more nor less than this, namely, that Parliament thus defined has, under the English constitution, the right to make or unmake any law whatever; and further, that no person or body is recognised by the law of England as having a right to override or set aside the legislation of Parliament.[2]

By virtue of supremacy, no Parliament is bound by its predecessor.

His definition of the rule of law has also 'had a profound influence among those who think and write about the constitution, as well as those who work it'.[3] For him, the concept comprised three 'distinct though kindred conceptions'. First, there was the supremacy of regular law as opposed to arbitrary power. Second, no one was above the law, with everyone subject to the law of the land and amenable to the jurisdiction of the ordinary tribunals. Third, the general principles of the constitution, such as personal liberty and the right of public meeting, were the result of judicial decisions determining the rights of private persons in cases brought before the courts.[4]

Understanding both is necessary to make sense of the UK constitution. However, there are two problems. One is that the definition of the rule of law is contested. The other is that, despite Dicey's claim as to their kindred nature, they are not necessarily compatible with one another. Who wins in the event of the conflict?

The rule of law

Dicey's definition has been variously challenged.[5] The first of his three conceptions, which saw the prohibition on arbitrary power as extending to the use of discretionary power by government, has been criticised for being a principle of political action. What was being advanced was the view that government should not hold such powers, rather than a juridical principle governing the exercise of power.[6] However undesirable, discretionary powers can be conferred on public authorities. In terms of equal rights and duties under the law, various public authorities have powers denied to the ordinary citizen.[7] 'All public officials, and especially public authorities, have powers and therefore rights which are not possessed by other persons.'[8] Jennings took the view that Dicey meant that an official committing a tort, or civil wrong, would be liable for it in the civil courts. That, he asserted, was a small point 'upon which to base a doctrine called by the magnificent name of "rule of law", particularly when it is generally used in a very different sense'.[9] The third conception has been challenged on the grounds that it is not clear why it is kindred to the other two and because rights have been enacted or modified by statute. Insofar as it was stating that law protecting rights is judge-made, it was partially correct, but a statement of the obvious, and incorrect in that not all such law is judge-made. Rights may be created, extended or limited by statute. As Jennings observed, the law determines the constitution, though the constitution determines the law. 'The supremacy of Parliament *is* the Constitution.'[10]

The essential point is not the specifics on which Dicey's definition is challenged, but the very fact that there is no agreement as to the meaning. Some academics have argued that the concept covers only form and procedures (the rule-book, or 'content free', conception), whereas others, such as Ronald Dworkin, favour a rights, or 'content rich', definition, encompassing the enforcement of moral rights.[11] Lord Bingham observed that there are so many definitions that there is a temptation to see the term as meaningless.[12] He cites John Finnis' observation that the rule of law is the name 'commonly given to the state of affairs in which a legal system is legally in good shape'.[13] However, this is relevant in that the rule of law is a feature of liberal democracies (Chapter 1). Without constitutionalism, a culture accepting limits on authority and seeing the legal process as serving citizens, there is no rule of law.[14] There may be, as in the People's Republic of China, rule *by* law, but not the rule *of* law. According to US supreme court justice, Stephen Breyer, 'following the law is a matter of custom, of habit, of widely shared understandings as to how those in government and members of the public should … act when faced with a court decision they strongly dislike'.[15] The rule of law may thus be seen to encompass recognition of a real separation of the organs of the state, with an independent judiciary, and with rights respected and protected. 'The law guarantees everyone's individual freedoms against contraventions by government or other citizens. This can only happen if the legislature, executive and judiciary are separate. And a crucial element is an independent court system which is truly accessible to citizens.'[16]

This is germane for understanding how the UK constitution works. The judiciary is independent of the other branches of government. That is a necessary, but not a sufficient, condition for the rule of law. There is recognition by government that it must abide by judgments of the courts. Since the 1960s, there has been greater judicial activism on the part of the courts.[17] Judicial review of ministerial actions has been a marked feature of administrative justice. The courts have also gained a more prominent role as a result of the European Communities Act 1972 and the Human Rights Act 1998.

As a consequence of the UK's membership of the European Union, the courts have been able to hold provisions of UK law incompatible with EU law. The Human Rights Act enables senior courts to issue declarations of incompatibility where they determine that legislation or action of a public body falls foul of a provision of the European Convention on Human Rights (ECHR). The act confers no powers on the courts to strike a law down. Parliament could choose to ignore a declaration of incompatibility and not change the law to bring it into line with what the courts say it should be in order to be compatible with the ECHR. In practice, ministers have acted in such a way as to ensure that the UK is compliant with its obligations under the convention. On occasion a declaration of incompatibility, especially on anti-terrorism legislation, has not always been well received by ministers,[18] but ministers have nonetheless moved to amend legislation to bring it into line with judgments of the courts. For several years, government held out from acting on a declaration of incompatibility that a blanket ban on prisoners being able to vote was incompatible with convention rights[19] but eventually a compromise was reached to ensure that the UK remained compliant with its obligations under the ECHR. Ministers thus acted in a way they would have preferred not to act, but they did so because it was their obligation, as they recognised it, to maintain the rule of law.

The significance of the concept, as well as the problems associated with it, is to be found in the provisions of the Constitutional Reform Act 2005. This removed the requirement for the lord chancellor, a cabinet minister, to be a senior lawyer and a member of the House of Lords. The lord chancellor was seen as someone who could serve within government as a voice for, and a protector of, the judiciary and uphold the rule of law. To compensate for this change, the government accepted amendments to the bill to provide that ministers 'must uphold the continued independence of the judiciary'[20] and the lord chancellor, under the oath of office, swears 'to respect the rule of law'.[21] The act thus acknowledges the rule of law, but the interpretation section of the act is silent as to the meaning of the term.

The concept of the rule of law is thus accepted as a key tenet of the British constitution, and is embodied now in law, but without any precise definition of the term. Certain features are seen as intrinsic to the concept, such as the independence of the judiciary, but the precise contours remain unclear.

Parliamentary sovereignty versus the rule of law

It follows from the very definition of parliamentary sovereignty that it constitutes what Gordon has described as 'the central organising principle of the UK constitution'.[22] While not all the legal powers exercised by organs of the state flow from what Parliament has determined, 'the legislative power of Parliament is hierarchically superior to all other constitutional authority'.[23] What flows from this is that '(i)n so far as Dicey's general statement of the rule of law may be taken to involve the existence in the English Constitution of certain principles almost amounting to fundamental laws, his doctrine is logically inconsistent with the legislative supremacy of Parliament'.[24] For Dicey it was parliamentary sovereignty *and* the rule of law. There is, though, as Bingham noted, the potential for conflict, parliamentary sovereignty *versus* the rule of law.[25]

Parliamentary sovereignty asserts that the outputs of Parliament are binding. It is legal sovereignty that is covered. Parliament could legislate to encroach on the rule of law. It does not do so, not because it cannot in law, but because it accepts it is constrained by political principle. It should not do so, therefore it does not do so. It is also limited in practice by the fact that citizens may refuse to comply with law. There is, as Dicey recognised, the potential for 'popular resistance'.[26] As Hood Phillips and Jackson observed,[27] in industrial relations, trade unions may resist attempts to limit the power of workers. There are thus limits, but not legal limits.

Parliament does not legislate to provide that judges give judgments favouring the crown because it would be morally wrong to do so. In essence, Parliament does not so much conflict with the rule of law as exist within it. It does not legislate to outlaw drinking alcohol because it would be unenforceable. It may be able to regulate the sale and consumption of alcohol in certain places, but it would be impossible to enforce it in the home. It could legislate to revoke the independence of former colonies such as India. The measures constitute United Kingdom law, but not law that would be enforceable in nations no longer subject to the crown.

The essential point therefore is that the two pillars normally co-exist peacefully. However, that does not mean they necessarily will do so continuously. What if there is a clash and Parliament legislates in a way seen by the courts to encroach on certain rights? Should not the courts enforce the law regardless? That would flow logically from Dicey's definition of parliamentary sovereignty. That the courts should enforce the outputs of Parliament under the doctrine of parliamentary sovereign was and remains the predominant view of the judiciary. Recent years, however, have seen this doctrine questioned by some jurists, one, Lord Hope of Craighead asserting (in the *Axa* case, discussed below) that 'the rule of law enforced by the courts is the ultimate controlling factor on which our constitution is based'.

The differing views rest on conflicting interpretations of the basis of parliamentary sovereignty. Some lawyers see it as a judicially self-imposed doctrine. 'The doctrine of legislative supremacy is a doctrine of the common law. Like any other rule of the common law it may be developed, refined, re-interpreted, or even changed by the judges.'[28] It was confirmed by the glorious revolution in that the courts accepted that Parliament had triumphed over the crown and that acts of the crown-in-Parliament trumped decisions of the courts.[29] Before then, the doctrine had not gone unchallenged. In *Dr Bonham's Case* in 1610, the lord chief justice, Lord Coke, said, in a much-quoted comment, that 'when an Act of Parliament is against common right and reason, or repugnant, or impossible to be performed, the common law will control it, and adjudge such Act to be void'. Various authorities argued that there was a 'common law constitution', with the crown and Parliament limited by ancient powers.[30]

Jeffrey Goldsworthy has shown that perceptions of a common law constitution were unfounded. Common law never subjected the legislative authority of Parliament to limits that could justify the courts invalidating an act of Parliament.[31] It is not clear that common law was viewed in the way that it is now conceived. (Even Coke departed from his view in the *Dr Bonham Case*.) It is possible that it was seen as custom that was interpreted by the high court of Parliament and not by inferior courts.[32] Parliament cannot by an act of Parliament legislate for parliamentary sovereignty because that would be to confer the very power being acted upon. Similarly, though, the courts cannot confer authority on themselves. 'It follows that their authority cannot come from the common law, if this is judge-made law.'[33] Dicey, as we have noted, identified two fundamental features that have characterised political institutions of England since Norman times. The key point is that power derived from the sovereign, which then was exercised through the crown-in-Parliament. This is the ultimate authority and the courts have worked within that. Judicial acceptance is necessary, but it is not sufficient; judges cannot unilaterally change the legal rules.[34]

The consistent and prevailing view of parliamentary sovereignty was expressed by Lord Bingham in *The Rule of Law* (2010). He argued that the doctrine of parliamentary sovereignty was not the creation of judges under the common law and therefore not something that could be adjusted by judges as they saw fit. To him, parliamentary sovereignty was immanent in the United Kingdom's constitution and could only be altered by a whole new constitutional settlement.[35] As he wrote:

> The British people have not repelled the extraneous power of the papacy in spiritual matters and the pretensions of royal power in temporal in order to subject themselves to the unchallengeable rulings of unelected judges.[36]

The judges did not establish the principle of parliamentary sovereignty so it was not open to them to change it. However, although this remains the dominant view, it is not the exclusive view of jurists.

Some judges in recent years have raised the issue of whether courts could strike down legislation. The claim that parliamentary sovereignty was a principle of common law, and could therefore be modified by the courts, was made by Lord Justice Laws in 2002 in *Thorburn* v. *Sunderland City Council*, known as the 'metric martyr case'. In his *obiter dictum*, he advanced the view that there were certain acts that were of such constitutional importance that they could only be changed by express, and not implied, repeal. These included the European Communities Act 1972, the Human Rights Act 1998, and the measures providing for devolution. There was thus a 'hierarchy of Acts of Parliament'. A 'constitutional' statute was one if it '(a) conditions the legal relationship between citizens and state in some general, overarching manner, or (b) enlarges or diminishes the scope of what we would now regard as fundamental constitutional rights'. What flowed from the distinction was that constitutional acts could not be impliedly repealed, whereas ordinary acts could. This distinction could not derive from Parliament, since it could not stipulate the manner of future legislation, but it was an invention of the common law. For Lord Bridge in *Factortame (No. 2)*, EU law enjoyed primacy over domestic law by virtue of the actions of Parliament. Here, Laws was advancing an argument that it derived from a judicial determination of a hierarchy of law. As Gordon observed, 'if it is the case that the courts are constitutionally entitled, under the guise of a variation in the common law, to amend unilaterally the conditions by which Parliament's ultimate legislative authority must be exercised, the doctrine of parliamentary sovereignty will have been replaced with one of judicial supremacy'.[37]

Further cases generated *obiter dicta* that called into question more directly the supremacy of the doctrine. The *Jackson* case in 2005 involved a challenge to the validity of the Hunting Act 2004, banning foxhunting, which had been enacted under the provisions of the Parliament Act 1949 after the House of Lords had failed to pass the bill. The claimants argued that the Parliament Act 1949, having been passed under the provisions of the Parliament Act 1911, had the status of subordinate legislation and had not been validly enacted. They argued that the House of Commons, as one element of the crown-in-Parliament, could not increase its own powers, as it had done by virtue of the 1949 act. The law lords rejected the argument on the basis that the provisions of the 1911 act stipulated that any measure passed under its provisions would have the status of an act of Parliament. They also took the view that the act limited the powers of the House of Lords rather than enlarging the powers of the House of Commons.

The decision in the case, according to Michael Gordon, reinforced the doctrine,[38] although the very fact that the highest court heard the case could be seen as a challenge to it. Under the doctrine it is not within the gift of the courts to question acts of Parliament: it is their task to administer acts, not question whether they should be on the statute book. However, the case is significant not so much for the judgment, which upheld the doctrine, but for *dicta* that queried it and conveyed that there may be occasions when the courts may not recognise acts that prescribed flagrant abuses of power. Both Lord Steyn and Lord Hope of Craighead advanced the view that parliamentary sovereignty was, in Lord Steyn's words, 'a construct of the common law'. According to Steyn: 'The classic account given by Dicey of the doctrine of the supremacy of Parliament, pure and absolute as it was, can now be seen to be out of place in the modern United Kingdom.'[39] The doctrine was still the 'general' principle of the constitution and the principle one created by judges. 'If that is so', he continued, 'it is not unthinkable that circumstances could arise where the courts may have to qualify a principle established on a different hypothesis of constitutionalism'. In exceptional cases, such as an attempt to abolish judicial review, the highest court 'may have to consider whether this is [a] constitutional fundamental which even a sovereign Parliament acting at the behest of a complaisant House of Commons cannot abolish'.

Lord Hope advanced a similar line of argument, contending that 'parliamentary sovereignty is no longer, if it ever was, absolute … It is no longer right to say that its freedom to legislate admits of no qualification whatever'.[40] Baroness Hale opined that the courts 'will treat with particular suspicion (and might even reject) any attempt to subvert the rule of law by removing governmental action affecting the rights of the individual from all judicial scrutiny'.[41] A majority – seven out of nine law lords – also supported *dicta* that the Parliament Acts could not be employed to pass an act that removed the provision in the 1911 act (section 2(1)) excluding a measure to extend the life of a Parliament. Lord Bingham, in the minority, recognised that there was nothing in the language of section 2(1) that would support the argument that it was unamendable save with the consent of the House of Lords.

In the *Axa* case in 2011, a challenge was mounted to an act of the Scottish Parliament on the grounds that it was outside the legislative competence of the Parliament. The supreme court held that it was not outside competence, nor that it was incompatible (as the claimants had argued) with the ECHR. It also rejected the argument that acts of the Scottish Parliament were reviewable on common law grounds of irrationality, unreasonableness or arbitrariness. Lord Hope opined, though, that review may be required in 'exceptional circumstances'. He also used the occasion to reiterate what he said in *Jackson*, namely 'that the rule of law enforced by the courts is the ultimate controlling factor on which our constitution is based'.[42] A government could use the power to abolish judicial review – 'Whether this is likely to happen is not the point. It is enough that it might conceivably do so' – and therefore the rule of law 'requires that the judges must retain the power to insist that legislation of that extreme kind is not the law which the courts will recognise'.[43]

Lord Hope's view fundamentally challenges the Diceyian view and that advanced by Lord Bingham. That a government would not use such a power is, in Diceyian terms, not beside the point – quite the reverse – and it is not a case of judges retaining a power, since they did not have it in the first place. There was therefore nothing to retain.

Although these views were in the form of opinion – they were not part of the reasoning (the *ratio decindi*) in each case – they were sufficient to concern ministers and Parliament. As Alison Young noted, they appear to have motivated, at least in part, the 'sovereignty clause' (section 18) of the European Union Act 2011.[44] The section provided that directly effective EU law, under section 2(1) of the European Communities Act 1972, 'falls to be recognised and available in law in the United Kingdom only by virtue of that Act or where it is required to be recognised and available in law by virtue of any other Act'. This was designed to protect the doctrine of parliamentary sovereignty from erosion if the courts were to consider EU law entrenched in the legal system as part of the common law. In speaking to the provision when the bill was going through the Commons, the minister for Europe made clear that it was motivated by the opinions of Lord Justice Laws in *Thorburn* and Lord Steyn in *Jackson*. It was also prompted by the risk of further challenges to the claim that EU law gains direct effect in the UK through the operation of a UK statute.[45]

Although Parliament provided for the repeal of the European Communities Act upon the UK's exit from membership of the European Union, the *obiter dicta* of the judges challenging the doctrine of parliamentary sovereignty as superior to common law is independent of that development. The *Thorburn, Jackson* and *Axa* cases are important not so much for what was decided, but for what was said unrelated to the reasoning for the decisions. The *obiter* of the judges – Laws, Steyn and Hope – represents a notable minority view among jurists. However, their views raise fundamental issues as to the nature of the relationship of Dicey's twin pillars.

This matters for the reasons advanced by Elliott and Feldman. If there was a clash between Parliament and the courts, 'no constitutional roadmap determines what would happen in the event of such a showdown. The obvious risk arises … that the courts might end up the losers in an institutional standoff with Parliament'.[46] Then again, they may not. This very fact encourages some element of self-restraint on both sides. The possibility of institutional tension, as Elliott and Feldman note, also 'demands a form of institutional comity that requires legislative respect for fundamental constitutional values as well as judicial respect for Parliament's legislative authority'.[47] As they go on to note:

> In the absence of textually demarcated constitutional domains, each organ has a vested interest in securing its own territory by preserving the *status quo*, including by according to other organs respect whose withdrawal would likely precipitate a constitutional crisis with unpredictable results. Viewed from the perspective of the legislative branch, this, in itself, can plausibly be characterised as a

restraint upon its authority, notwithstanding that the form of any such restraint is other than straightforwardly legal.[48]

The extent to which there is comity will be considered later (Chapter 6). Absent comity, there is the potential of the fundamentals of the constitution unravelling. If the 'central organising principle' of the constitution is contested and ceases to apply, the result is a constitutional quagmire.

Notes

1   Dicey 1959: 184.
2   Dicey 1959: 39–40.
3   Hood Phillips and Jackson 1978: 36; see also Jennings 1959: 305.
4   Dicey 1959: 188, 193, 195.
5   Norton 1982: 15–16.
6   Jennings 1959: 307–11.
7   Hood Phillips and Jackson 1978: 37.
8   Jennings 1959: 312.
9   Jennings 1959: 312.
10 Jennings 1959: 314.
11 Le Sueur *et al.* 2016: 91–4.
12 Bingham 2010: 6.
13 Finnis 1980: 270.
14 See Bingham 2010: 9.
15 Quoted in Corstens 2017: 3.
16 Corstens 2017: 2.
17 Norton 1982: 135–42.
18 See Chapter 6 and Norton 2015a: 59–61.
19 Norton 2015a: 58–9.
20 Constitutional Reform Act 2005, s3;1.
21 Constitutional Reform Act 2005, s17.
22 Gordon 2015: 23.
23 Gordon 2015: 23.
24 Hood Phillips and Jackson 1978: 39.
25 Bingham 2010: 168–70.
26 Dicey 1959: 76.
27 Hood Phillips and Jackson 1978: 37–8.
28 Tompkins 2003: 103.
29 Tompkins 2003: 104.

30 Goldsworthy 2010: 18–19.
31 Goldsworthy 2010: 19; see Goldsworthy 1999.
32 Goldsworthy 2010: 22.
33 Goldsworthy 2010: 51.
34 Goldsworthy 2010: 54–5; see also Elliott 2002: 362–76.
35 See Dickson 2019: 64.
36 Bingham 2010: 168.
37 Gordon 2015: 167.
38 Gordon 2015: 194–201.
39 [2005] UK House of Lords (UKHL) 56, [2006] 1 Appeal Court (AC) 262: 102.
40 *Jackson*, 104.
41 *Jackson*, 159.
42 [2011] UK Supreme Court (UKSC) 46, 51.
43 *Axa*, 51.
44 Young 2017: 200.
45 *House of Commons Debates* (*HC Deb.*) 11 January 2011, col. 244.
46 Elliott and Feldman 2015: 79–80.
47 Elliott and Feldman 2015: 80.
48 Elliott and Feldman 2015: 80.

Chapter 3

Constitutional conventions: when is a convention not a convention?

The formal provisions of a constitution, enshrined in legally enforceable form, are necessary, but they are not sufficient to ensure the smooth running of the state. They need some lubricant to work efficiently. They rely for this on conventions and practices. Constitutional conventions, as we noted in Chapter 1, are ubiquitous. 'They can be found in all constitutions.'[1]

The meaning of conventions is contested. The most useful and authoritative definition is that they are rules of behaviour that have no legal force, but which are deemed to be binding on those at whom they are directed.[2] They are thus distinguishable from law[3] and practice.[4] They constitute moral obligations – they are complied with because they are right behaviour.[5] Law is enforced by forces external to the individual. Conventions are self-enforced. Given that they are morally justified, they are met on an invariable basis. Rules that are departed from on occasion, or are qualified in expression, or enforced by others, do not qualify as conventions.

Some works have adopted a looser definition, taking conventions as informal rules generally agreed by actors in the political system. This has enabled Heard to identify a hierarchy of 'conventions': fundamental, meso- and semi-, and infra-conventions and usages.[6] The qualifications inherent in these terms mean they constitute practices. Feldman distinguishes law and non-legal constitutional norms, but argues that there is 'no clear water' between different types of norms.[7] We treat conventions as distinct from practices and from rules, duties and expectations that are enforceable by some external sanction. Ministers may work within the context of expectations,[8] but expectations may not always be met.

Conventions differ from law not only in the form of enforcement, but also in the nature of expression. Legislation requires precision. If an intention cannot be rendered in clear legal form, parliamentary counsel will advise government that it cannot be done. Some conventions, as we shall see, have clear meaning and associated boundaries, but the contours of others are imprecise. We shall address the rare occasions when conventions have been transposed into statute. The exercise of rendering some in precise legal form has proved a fraught exercise.

It is possible for behaviour to be invariable without constituting a convention. Some behaviour may be uniform for political reasons. Some authorities inferred from the absence of government defeats in the House of Commons division lobbies, at least for a period in the mid-twentieth century, that it was a convention that a government had to resign if it was defeated in any vote.[9] This view had no basis in fact nor in any original authoritative source. Defeat in itself did not demonstrate a loss of confidence in the government[10] and therefore did not engage the convention governing confidence, which we consider below. Prior to the Fixed-Term Parliaments Act 2011, which removed the queen's residual powers in respect of dissolution, the monarch acceded to a prime minister's request for a general election. However, it was recognised that adhering to the request may not be met in all circumstances.[11] Determining what those circumstances are is not clear-cut.[12] The king's private secretary, Sir Alan Lascelles, wrote anonymously to *The Times* in 1950 identifying certain conditions under which a request for a dissolution may be refused.[13]

Conventions develop through different routes.[14] One is the assertion of a moral principle that is then confirmed in invariable behaviour. One instance of this, considered below, is the Salisbury convention. They may develop the other way round, with practice developing and being accepted as morally correct by those who engage in it. The other examples we consider below fall in this category. With this category, there is the difficulty of establishing at what point behaviour, underpinned by a moral imperative, acquires the status of a convention. What Jaconelli terms the 'birth' of a convention may take time and be complicated. That the prime minister should sit in the House of Commons, discussed below, is a case in point.

Given this, it is perhaps not surprising that there is no formal, and certainly no immutable, list of the conventions that have developed. Geoffrey Marshall offered a wide-ranging analysis in his *Constitutional Conventions* (1984), embracing conventions in different spheres, encompassing not just the crown and ministers, but also other holders of public office, extending to the police and the army. In 2006, a joint committee of both Houses of Parliament examined the conventions that govern the relationship between the two Houses.[15] What is notable about both studies is how much of what was examined did not meet the criteria to be deemed conventions, but rather constituted practice.

There are, though, several conventions that are clearly core to the effective operation of the political system. We address the principal ones as well as one that may be developing.

Key conventions

Constitutional principles provide the basis for conventions.[16] A number of conventions derive from a core principle of the constitution, namely that for the monarchy to symbolise the unity of the nation, the monarch has to stand above politics. The monarch now forms what Walter Bagehot, in *The English Constitution* in 1867, termed the 'dignified' part of the constitution.[17] Queen Victoria's reign marked the transition from a monarchy playing some role in politics to one rising above it. The position was confirmed in the twentieth century. 'Since 1901 the trend toward a real political neutrality, not merely a matter of appearances, has been steady reign by reign.'[18]

The principle generates obligations on the part of both the monarch and ministers. Those borne by the monarch are long-standing. The clearest – there is no ambiguity as to its contours – as well as the most well established is that the monarch assents to bills passed by both Houses of Parliament, thus ensuring the monarch exercises no political judgment on the merits of the measure. The last occasion a monarch exercised a veto was in March 1708, when Queen Anne vetoed the 1707 Scottish Militia Bill. Her predecessor, William III, had occasionally exercised a veto – his vetoes being more controversial than Anne's – but its use barely survived the glorious revolution.

The detachment of the monarch is marked also by the prerogative being exercised on the advice of ministers. That ministers exercise powers in the name of the crown is made apparent by announcements emanating directly from those taking the decisions. The declaration of war in 1939 was announced not by the king, but by Prime Minister Neville Chamberlain. The decision to commit British forces to retake the Falkland Islands in 1982, following the invasion by Argentinian forces, was made in, and announced from, 10 Downing Street.

The convention that the monarch acts on the advice of ministers is mirrored by the moral obligation accepted by ministers that they must not offer advice that would bring the sovereign into the territory of political controversy. The problem here is in knowing that would be the effect of their advice. The queen was put in a potentially embarrassing political situation in 1957 and more especially 1963 when a new leader of the Conservative Party did not 'emerge' under the party's process for determining a leader. However, the problem in this instance was the absence of clear procedures. The selection of the prime minister is one (and now the only) prerogative power which is not formally exercised on advice. The queen may seek advice, but she is not bound by it. In 1963, faced with Harold Macmillan's sudden resignation, and with no one successor having emerged, she sought Macmillan's advice. He provided a memorandum, which embodied the results of soundings taken of cabinet ministers and most Conservative MPs, as well as of constituency parties.[19] She acted on the basis of the advice. The selection generated controversy. Although criticism was directed primarily at leading figures in the Conservative Party – Bogdanor believes that criticism of the queen lacked substance and that she 'acted perfectly constitutionally'[20] – it was unhelpful to the monarch inasmuch as it was seen as showing 'disrespect for the royal prerogative'.[21] The Conservative Party after 1963 moved quickly to adopt a new procedure so that such a situation could not arise again (see Chapter 9). When the 2010 general election failed to produce a clear outcome and negotiations took place between parties with a view to forming a coalition, the queen was kept informed of events, but was quite clearly detached from them. When agreement was reached on a Conservative–Liberal Democrat coalition, Labour Prime Minister Gordon Brown immediately went to the palace to resign and to advise the queen to send for David Cameron. Such actions reflected a wider obligation on politicians, not simply Her Majesty's ministers. The moral obligation, though, is most clearly one shouldered by the prime minister as the sovereign's principal adviser.

In short, the queen by convention acts on the advice of her prime minister. By convention, the prime minister does not offer advice that would jeopardise the position of the sovereign.

It is a convention that the prime minister serves in the House of Commons. Since the development of the office of prime minister, the holder has served in either the Lords or the Commons, sometimes moving, as happened in the case of Benjamin Disraeli, from the Commons to the Lords. However, it developed as a convention in the twentieth century that the prime minister must be an MP. The origins of this are to be found in the events of 1923, when the prime minister, Bonar Law, who was dying of throat cancer, resigned. There were two leading contenders to replace him, MP Stanley Baldwin and Lord Curzon. Curzon was the more senior of the two and expected to be summoned. In the event, he was summoned to London, but for the purpose of being informed that Baldwin was being appointed prime minister.

The reason for George V summoning Baldwin was not primarily on the grounds that a prime minister could no longer be drawn from the unelected House, though that was a consideration, but was more specific to the political situation at the time. In the general election of the previous year, the Labour Party had emerged as the official opposition, eclipsing the Liberal Party. The Liberal Party had a sizeable, albeit minority, body of peers. The Labour Party did not. The Lords was bereft of Labour members. The king took the view that it would thus be difficult to have a prime minister serve in a House where he would not be open to question and challenge by the official opposition.[22] He sought advice, which both coincided with his view and tended to favour Baldwin,[23] so involved no conflict with what he deemed the appropriate course of action.

Drawing the prime minister from the Commons clearly became the practice, but the fact that it was not yet a convention appears borne out by the events of 1940. After Neville Chamberlain's decision to resign as prime minister, there was some resistance among Conservative MPs to Winston Churchill being appointed as his successor. Chamberlain, and the king, favoured Lord Halifax, the foreign secretary.[24] Halifax demurred. Although being in the Lords was offered as the official reason, Halifax recorded that it was primarily because he recognised that he lacked Churchill's qualities and as defence secretary Churchill would be in an extremely powerful position, rendering Halifax little more than an honorary prime minister.[25] The Labour Party would have been prepared to accept Halifax: Hugh Dalton saw no objection to the 'Lords difficulty'. In the circumstances, 'there was nothing to stop

Parliament in the crisis of war from passing an *ad hominem* Act allowing Halifax to answer questions and speak, if not vote, in the Commons. There would have been no serious opposition to such a measure, if Halifax had wished to be Prime Minister'.[26] His membership of the Lords was thus not seen as a conclusive bar to him becoming prime minister. 'None of those favouring Halifax saw any *constitutional* objections to a Prime Minister in the House of Lords'.[27]

Two decades later, that stance had gone. It was no longer seen as constitutionally proper for the occupant of No. 10 to serve, or at least remain, in the Lords. When in 1963 the Earl of Home was summoned to form a government, he promptly renounced his peerage (made possible by the Peerages Act 1963) and gained election to the House of Commons in a by-election. The convention is thus not that the prime minister must necessarily be drawn from the Commons, but that to serve as prime minister he or she must sit in the Commons. The likelihood of the person chosen not already being in the Commons is, though, now remote, given the rules adopted by the major parties for the election of their leaders. Candidature is confined to MPs. Although the parties may bind themselves,[28] the monarch is not formally bound by those rules. Her choice is determined by convention.

Another convention that developed in the twentieth century is the Salisbury convention. This has its origins in a speech made by the Conservative leader in the Lords, Viscount Cranborne, on 16 August 1945 in which he declared that measures embodied in the manifesto of the party winning a general election should not be rejected by the House of Lords. This was the logical consequence of the referendal theory developed by his grandfather, the 3rd Marquess of Salisbury, following the 1867 Reform Act. Salisbury argued that the House of Lords was entitled to reject a measure and refer it to the people, through an election, if it did not clearly have the consent of the people.[29] What had been fashioned to limit Liberal governments in the nineteenth century was now used to sustain the measures of a Labour government in the twentieth. The House of Lords ever since has not rejected on second reading or agreed a wrecking amendment to a bill envisaged in the government's election manifesto. The convention also extends to a manifesto bill being sent to the Commons so that it has reasonable time to consider it or any amendments proffered by the Lords. However, the contours here are less precise: what constitutes 'reasonable time' has never been clearly defined.

A more recent instance of a practice developing into a convention is that governing when UK military forces are committed to action abroad. Prior to the twenty-first century, governments used the prerogative to commit forces to action, as in the Second World War, and then reported to the Commons and answered for their actions. This changed early in the new century. In 2003, Prime Minister Tony Blair set a precedent when he sought the approval of the House of Commons for UK forces to be deployed in action in Iraq. The war was highly controversial and split Labour MPs, but authorisation was achieved, with opposition support, by 412 votes to 149. It was, according to Tony Blair, 'the only military action expressly agreed in advance by the House of Commons'.[30] In August 2013, Prime Minister David Cameron sought approval for committing forces in Syria, but the government suffered a defeat by 285 votes to 272. 'It is very clear tonight', Cameron said, 'that, while the House has not passed a motion, the British Parliament, reflecting the views of the British people, does not want to see British military action. I get that, and the Government will act accordingly'.[31]

Some commentators took the view that it had become a convention that no government could embark on military action without first getting the endorsement of the House of Commons.[32] However, in 2018, Prime Minister Theresa May authorised air strikes in Syria, in conjunction with the United States and France, without seeking prior parliamentary approval. She justified her action on the grounds that revealing the plans for action 'would have fundamentally undermined the effectiveness of their action and endangered the security of our American and French allies'.[33]

The distinction is between action that cannot be revealed for fear of jeopardising an operation and that which can be considered openly. Seeking support of the Commons in the latter situation may be deemed now a convention, but the problems of distinguishing between the categories is such that Gordon Brown as prime minister was frustrated in his attempt to formalise the war powers convention through either a motion or legislation. This case illustrates that the contours of conventions may be vague. As we shall see, attempts to transpose conventions into precise rules through statute can be a fraught exercise.

Not a convention?

Conventions are, then, core to the constitution, but there can be difficulties in establishing when they exist. When is a convention not a convention? There are occasions when a practice is mistaken for a convention. There are occasions also when conventions cease to be such when they are transposed into statute and when they are broken.

A practice, not a convention. Confusion exists because some practices are titled as conventions. Two examples are to be found in the Sewel 'convention' and the 'convention' governing approval of statutory instruments by the House of Lords. Both fail the test in that neither establishes a rule that is unqualified.

The Sewel convention derives from a statement made by Scottish Office minister, Lord Sewel, during passage of the Scotland Bill in 1998, namely that the UK Parliament will not normally legislate for Scotland without the consent of the Scottish Parliament. It was, though, not a convention by virtue of the qualification ('normally'). The government thus left open the possibility that it could legislate without the approval of the Scottish

Parliament. Formally, Parliament could do that anyway. However, stating that Parliament would never legislate without the consent of the Scottish Parliament would have put the government in a political, if not a legal, bind. It would invite accusations of betrayal if it proceeded with legislation affecting Scotland without the Parliament at Holyrood passing a legislative consent (originally known as a Sewel) motion inviting it to extend it in this way. It thus left itself an escape clause.

It is the practice of the House of Lords not to reject statutory instruments laid by the government. This practice has been assumed by some to constitute a convention. In 2015, a review was undertaken by former cabinet minister Lord Strathclyde at the request of Prime Minister David Cameron after the House of Lords voted to delay approval of a statutory instrument on tax credits. According to a Downing Street spokesperson, 'The prime minister is determined we will address this constitutional issue. A convention exists and it has been broken. He has asked for a rapid review to see how it can be put back in place'.[34] The problem with the statement was that there was no convention to be broken.[35] In his review, Lord Strathclyde opened by defining a convention – 'non statutory but binding on those who come to agree them'[36] – but then departed from it in his consideration of what had happened. 'Since 1968', he declared, 'a convention has existed that the House of Lords should not reject statutory instruments (or should do so only rarely)',[37] thus injecting the sort of qualification found in the Sewel convention. In short, the 'convention' was binding on the Lords except on those occasions when it departed from it. Given that the Lords has asserted 'its unfettered freedom to vote on any subordinate legislation submitted for its consideration',[38] there is clearly no moral obligation accepted on its part to approve such legislation on an invariable basis. The review examined different options for limiting the power of the House of Lords in dealing with statutory instruments, but no action resulted from it.

Converting into statute. On occasion, a convention is translated into statute. Such transposition is rare, not least because statute law requires precision. Conventions do not always lend themselves to such precision.

There are three notable instances of conventions being transposed into statute. One is the Parliament Act 1911, providing that money bills passed by the House of Commons are enacted into law without the consent of the House of Lords. (Money bills are concerned only with national taxation, public money or loans and certified as such by the Speaker.) This is a consequence of the House of Lords departing from the convention that it did not reject finance bills and voting down on second reading Lloyd George's finance bill in 1909. Although the Lords retained the power to reject (though not amend) such bills, it had not done so for 200 years. The development of a mass franchise in the nineteenth century, enabling MPs to claim to speak for the people, strengthened the moral imperatives underpinning the convention. The rejection by the Lords of the 1909 budget triggered a constitutional crisis and the passage of the Parliament Bill in 1911, after the king agreed to the prime minister's request to accede to the creation of several hundred Liberal peers should that be necessary in order to provide a majority to get the measure passed.

A more problematic transposition is to be found in the Fixed-Term Parliaments Act 2011. Prior to its enactment, it was a convention that if the government lost the confidence of the House of Commons, the prime minister either sought a general election or tendered the government's resignation. The preference, on the rare occasions it lost a confidence vote, was to seek a general election.

The confidence of the House could be tested in three ways.[39] One was through voting on an explicit motion of no confidence. If the leader of the opposition tabled such a motion, the government by convention found time for it to be debated. The second was through a motion of confidence, typically moved by the government after the loss of a major vote on a policy issue. A government with an overall majority could normally ensure a vote of no confidence was rejected and a vote of confidence carried. The third way was through the prime minister attaching confidence to a vote on a specific issue, such as the second reading of a bill, and making clear that, if defeated on the motion, a general election would ensue. Edward Heath, for example, made the second reading of the European Communities Bill in 1972 a vote of confidence. Attaching confidence to a vote in this way is a means of maximising the governing party's voting strength. Some commentators also considered that losing votes on a major issue, such as the budget, would amount to an implicit vote of no confidence, but were this to happen it would be tantamount to falling in the third category, given that for the government to seek an election would be conceding it was a confidence vote. The government could decide not to treat it as such, but rather seek an explicit vote of confidence consequent to the defeat. Given this, defeat on a major issue is not a distinct category.

The Fixed-Term Parliaments Bill sought to transpose this convention into statute. The bill as introduced stipulated that it was for the Speaker to certify when the House had passed a motion of no confidence; and, once passed, if within fourteen days a government had not achieved passage of a motion of confidence, a general election would take place. The bill did not define what constituted a vote of no confidence. The government took the view that it would follow the convention, the terms of which it considered well understood, but under pressure agreed to it being specified in detail, removing ambiguity as to the conditions under which an election could be triggered.[40] As we shall see in Chapter 8, the act has given rise to significant problems that were not anticipated. The government can still designate a vote as one of confidence, and can resign in the event of a defeat, but it cannot opt for a general election. All it can do is call for one, as it did (successfully) in 2017 and on three occasions (unsuccessfully) in 2019.

The vote on the House of Commons taking control of the parliamentary timetable on 3 September 2019, to facilitate passage of the European Union Withdrawal (No. 2) Act, was treated, in effect, as a confidence vote for the purpose of taking the whip away from twenty-one Conservative MPs who voted against the government. The leader of the House, Jacob Rees-Mogg, argued that while the House was not willing to pass a motion of no confidence in the government, 'it tries to take away confidence on specifics while maintaining confidence in the generality. That is not a proper constitutional position to be in'.[41] The following day, the government moved a motion, under section 2 of the Fixed-Term Parliaments Act, for an early general election. The opposition abstained, with the result that the motion failed to achieve the required two-thirds majority.

The third instance is transposing the convention governing treaty-making powers. Negotiating and ratifying treaties is a prerogative power undertaken by government. However, under the Ponsonby rule, deriving from a statement in 1924 by foreign affairs minister, Arthur Ponsonby, and followed consistently by government since 1929, treaties were published and laid before Parliament as command papers and then twenty-one sitting days elapsed before ratification took place. Should a request be made to debate a treaty within the twenty-one days, the government acceded to the request. Both Houses also considered legislation that was necessary to give effect in UK law to treaty obligations.

The Public Administration Committee in the House of Commons, among other bodies, recommended that treaties, especially treaties with significant financial, legal, or territorial implications, should be subject to parliamentary debate and approval.[42] The government under Gordon Brown sought to give effect to the proposal as part of its *Governance of Britain* agenda. Under the Constitutional Reform and Governance Act 2010, treaties are to be ratified if within twenty-one sitting days neither House has resolved that the treaty shall not be ratified. If the House of Commons votes against ratification, and persists in voting against, the treaty is not ratified. Provision is made for exceptional cases, though in such cases ratification is prohibited if either House has already resolved that the treaty should not be ratified. The government also accepted an amendment (moved by this writer) that a treaty had to be accompanied by an explanatory memorandum explaining the provisions of the treaty and the reasons for seeking its ratification.

Putting the Ponsonby rule on a statutory basis has meant that about 30–35 treaties each year fall within the purview of the law. However, few treaties are of major political significance and, under the Ponsonby rule, a debate could have been triggered and, if both Houses objected, it was unlikely ratification would have taken place. It was also open to either House to refuse to enact the legislation necessary to give effect in UK law to a treaty's provisions. Since the 2010 act, no attempt has been made to prevent ratification of a treaty under its provisions. Were there to be such an attempt, there is a practical problem in that it would rely on government finding time for a debate.

In practical terms, therefore, converting the convention into statutory form has had no discernible effect and the process has been described by the House of Lords constitution committee as 'limited and flawed'.[43] This has potential implications for future years given that one consequence of UK withdrawal from the European Union is that treaties, not least trade treaties, will become more significant, both quantitatively and qualitatively.

Problems of transposition are perhaps even starkly shown by the fate of the Sewel 'convention'. As we have noted, the Sewel convention, in the way it was framed (by Lord Sewel), was a practice and not a convention. Its status became more confused when it was included in the Scotland Act 2016. Section 2 of the act has the heading 'Sewel convention'. Its inclusion creates an inherent contradiction. By virtue of its enactment, it is part of statute law, but it is included under the heading of the Sewel convention. Furthermore, it incorporates the words as originally enunciated by Lord Sewel, so it is not so much converting a convention into statute as stating a practice. In the *Miller* case in 2016, the UK supreme court said that, as section 2 embodied a convention, 'policing the scope and manner of its operation does not lie within the constitutional remit of the judiciary'. This applied also to the incorporation of the 'convention' in the Wales Act 2017. The result is a constitutional Alice in Wonderland situation, with a practice being incorporated in an act of Parliament under the heading of a convention, but despite being in a statute is deemed legally unenforceable by the courts by virtue of its description as a convention.

It is perhaps not surprising, therefore, that attempts to transpose conventions into statute are rare. Conventions and statutes, as well as practices and statutes, are essentially different beasts.

Breaking the convention. The final instance where a convention ceases to be such is where it is broken. There are relatively few occasions where conventions have broken down, though some practices may have been mistaken for a broken convention.

What may be viewed as the most obvious case of a convention breaking down in recent years has been in respect of collective ministerial responsibility. We shall examine individual and collective responsibility in more detail in Chapter 11. As we shall see, to describe collective ministerial responsibility as a convention is problematic given that it comprises several elements, some of which have the character of conventions and others that are practices. The *Ministerial Code* refers to it not as a convention, but as a principle[44] and the obligation to comply with it derives from the code, ownership of which rests with the prime minister.[45] Compliance derives therefore from a duty imposed on ministers and not from an exclusive sense of moral obligation.

Rather, the clearest case of a convention coming under pressure was in 2019 after Boris Johnson succeeded to the premiership. There were two occasions when he was reported to have contemplated acting in such a way as to bring the monarch into the realms of political controversy and one occasion when advice did prove embarrassing.

There were media reports in 2019 that the prime minister may advise the queen to veto the European Union Withdrawal (No. 5) Bill that had been passed by both Houses against the wishes of the government. In response to these reports, several leading law professors wrote to *The Times* to point out that royal assent was so well established that it was now a formality. To advise against consent 'would presume a governmental power to override Parliament, yet it is in Parliament, not the Executive, that sovereignty resides'.[46] That rather glossed over the fact that Parliament constitutes the crown-in-Parliament, sovereignty residing in that entity and stipulating that the outputs of Parliament are binding (Chapter 2). Arguably, the queen, operating under advice, would not be seeking to override 'Parliament' any more than if the House of Lords rejected a measure it would be overriding Parliament. The House of Lords would not do so because it is, in respect of manifesto bills, constrained by convention. Ministers in this instance were also constrained by convention. As the authors of the letter noted, offering advice to veto a bill would compromise the position of the crown by drawing it into political controversy. This was the key constraint. It was incumbent on the prime minister not to offer advice that would compromise the position of the queen and, in the event, no such advice was proffered.

There were also media reports that the prime minister was considering refusing to comply with the requirement of the act to write seeking an extension of the negotiations to withdraw from the EU. Not only that, but that he would defy a court order to do so and defy the queen to dismiss him.[47] A failure to comply would be justiciable. For the queen's principal minister to stay resolutely in Downing Street in the face of an adverse court judgment would have the potential to embarrass the monarch. In the event, the issue did not arise. The prime minister complied with the provisions of the act.

There were also reports in 2019 that, if a motion of no confidence in the government was put and carried, the prime minister would sit out the fourteen-day period stipulated by the Fixed-Term Parliaments Act (see Chapter 8). There was no formal bar on his doing so, but the possibility was discussed of opposition parties agreeing a leading parliamentarian who could command a parliamentary majority to form a caretaker government and with that name then being conveyed to the queen. The expectation was that the prime minister would then resign in order to give that person an opportunity to form a government, and seek a vote of confidence, within the fourteen-day period. Boris Johnson was reported to have said he would defy the queen to dismiss him in such a situation.[48] No agreement was reached between the parties and no vote of no confidence carried, so again the issue was moot.

The occasion when the monarch was drawn into controversy was when the prime minister, through the privy council, advised the queen to prorogue Parliament for five weeks over summer 2019. Prorogation is the act of bringing a session of Parliament to a close. While Parliament is prorogued, no business can be transacted. Had prorogation been for a few days, as was usual, it would not have raised any queries. In the event, the moment the advice for a five-week prorogation was tendered, it attracted criticism. As we shall see (Chapter 6), the advice was held by the supreme court to be unlawful. It found that the prime minister had acted improperly to 'stymie' Parliament and that his advice to the queen was therefore unlawful. By virtue of being justiciable, no convention was involved. However, although the advice was justiciable, the circumstances of exercising it did embarrass the monarch. It is therefore arguable that the convention was broken, arguable because of the need for ministers to know of the likely effects of their actions. Ministers appeared more circumspect thereafter and, as we have seen, despite media reports that the prime minister may act in a way as to defy the convention, he failed to do so.

The occasions also served, perhaps counter-intuitively, to demonstrate the value of conventions. There is no legal requirement for the monarch to accept the advice of ministers. If ministers offered advice that was utterly perverse and an apparent abuse of power, there is the ultimate sanction of the monarch refusing to accept the advice. Doing so would constitute an existential threat to the monarchy, which is why the conventions exist, but the fact that it could happen may give ministers pause for thought before embarking on some utterly extreme path. The capacity of the monarch to say no is a form of constitutional nuclear deterrent. Whether the institution could survive launching a more tactical strike is unknown. An implied threat may suffice to restrain ministers.

Conclusion

Conventions are valuable in providing some structure to the political process without relying on the rigid formality of statute. They have developed over time and form the oil that enables the machinery of state to adapt to political circumstance. If the oil dries up or is removed, the machinery starts to work imperfectly, if it works at all. Conventions may be clear or have fuzzy contours, they may emerge fully formed or take time to be recognised, and they rest on key players adhering to moral imperatives that have no means of formal enforcement, but they are essential to make the constitution work.

Notes

1   Feldman 2013: 93.
2   Wheare 1951: 179; Marshall and Moodie 1967: 26; Hood Phillips and Jackson 1978: 104–5; Galligan and Brenton 2015: 8.
3   Morton 1991–2: 130–8, cited in Feldman 2013: 95; Aroney 2015: 24–50.
4   See Norton and Maer 2018: 130.
5   Feldman 2013: 95.

6   Heard 1989: 63–82, 2012: 319–38; see also Barry *et al.* 2019: 664–83.
7   Feldman 2013: 119.
8   See Feldman 2013: 110, and Chapter 11.
9   Norton 1978a: 360.
10   Norton 1978a: 360–78.
11   Marshall 1984: 35–42.
12   Brazier 2008: 102–3.
13   Letters, *The Times*, 2 May 1950.
14   Wheare 1951: 179–80; Jaconelli 2013: 121–2.
15   Joint Committee on Conventions 2006.
16   Feldman 2013: 97.
17   Bagehot 1963: 61.
18   Hardie 1970: 188; see also Bogdanor 1995: 32–41.
19   Horne 1989: 559–66.
20   Bogdanor 1995: 98.
21   Heasman 1967: 166.
22   Nicolson 1952: 376–8.
23   See especially Blake 1955: 525–6.
24   Roberts 2014: 4.
25   Roberts 2014: 277.
26   Blake 1993: 266; see also Roberts 2014: 4.
27   Wheeler-Bennett 1958: 444n.
28   Jaconelli 2013: 127.
29   Norton 2013d: 156–7.
30   Blair 2010: 428.
31   *HC Deb.* 29 August 2013, cols. 1555–6.
32   Strong 2014; Constitution Committee, House of Lords 2014.
33   *HC Deb.* 17 April 2018, col. 207.
34   *Guardian*, 26 October 2015.
35   See Public Administration and Constitutional Affairs Committee, House of Commons 2016: 9–10.
36   Strathclyde Review 2015: 3.
37   Strathclyde Review 2015: 5.
38   *House of Lords Debate (HL Deb.)* 20 October 1994, cols. 356–83.
39   Norton 1978a: 360–78.
40   Norton 2014: 211–16.
41   *HC Deb.* 3 September 2019, col. 99.
42   Public Administration Committee, House of Commons 2004.
43   Constitution Committee, House of Lords 2019: 12.
44   Cabinet Office 2019: 4.
45   See Feldman 2013: 102.
46   Letters, *The Times*, 3 April 2019.
47   *Independent*, 30 September 2019.
48   See *The Times*, 6 October 2019; *Independent*, 10 October 2019.

Chapter 4

The constitution, the EU and Brexit: who governs?

The United Kingdom became a member of the European Communities (EC) on 1 January 1973. Membership created problems in terms of adaptation to the basic tenets of the constitution. Under the Maastricht Treaty, ratified in 1993, the EC became the European Union. In 2016, following a referendum in which electors voted for the UK to leave the EU, the UK government began negotiations for the UK's withdrawal. Just as joining had proved politically contentious and constitutional problematic, the same applied forty-three years later to ending membership.

The UK had first applied to join the EC in 1963, but the application was vetoed by French President Charles de Gaulle. His departure from the presidency in 1969 removed a major obstacle, being succeeded by a president who was to prove amenable to UK membership. Negotiations were completed and in 1972 Parliament enacted the European Communities Act, providing the basis in UK law for membership. The act was not a measure of ratification. The Act of Accession was signed under prerogative powers.

Membership was achieved despite significant opposition from a minority of MPs, especially on the Conservative benches. The Labour opposition also opposed membership, not on principle, but on the basis of the terms negotiated. Not all Labour MPs accepted the party line. In October 1971, there was a six-day debate on a motion to agree the principle of joining on the basis of the arrangements that had been negotiated. A total of sixty-nine Labour MPs defied a three-line whip to vote for it. A further twenty abstained from voting. The Conservative government allowed a free vote: 248 Conservatives voted in favour and thirty-nine against.[1] However, when the European Communities Bill was going through the House, the principal split was on the Conservative side of the House, with a persistent minority, led by Enoch Powell and John Biffen, opposing it throughout its passage.[2]

The divisions within both parties, and the bitterness engendered by the debate, reflected wider divisions in the country. The issue had divided the parties, not only against one another, but also within themselves. Those divisions pre-dated the negotiations in 1972, essentially existing from the end of the Second World War onwards and reflected in attitudes to discussions leading to the Treaty of Rome forming the European Economic Community (the EEC) (the UK declined to participate) and in the initial application for membership. The divisions persisted throughout the 1970s and became more pronounced after a speech in Bruges in 1988 by Prime Minister Margaret Thatcher, attacking the concept of a supranational government capable of imposing its will on the member states.[3] Debate thereafter was notable for its intensity and bitterness.

The reasons advanced for joining were essentially political and economic. The EC was seen as providing a platform for the UK again to play a leading role on the world stage and, more altruistically, help bring together the nations of Europe. It would help provide a community-wide market. The Single European Act came into force on 1 July 1987, reforming the institutional structures and relationships within the EC (and between the community and nation states) to facilitate achieving a single market within the EC. The UK did not join for constitutional reasons. If anything, it joined despite the constitutional implications and not because of them.

The challenges of membership

The consequences for the UK's constitutional arrangements were not fully realised at the time of membership. Membership was significant for the UK constitution in two respects, political and judicial.

First, it transferred law-making powers to supra-national institutions. The fields in which the EC, later the EU, could legislate expanded with succeeding treaties. The powers also expanded, strengthening the position of the centre ('Brussels') in relation to the member states. The Single European Act strengthened the European Parliament and extended provision for qualified majority voting (QMV) in the Council of Ministers, thus making it difficult for a single nation to veto a proposal to which it was opposed. The Maastricht Treaty (later titled the Treaty on European Union), taking effect in 1993, created the European Union and introduced a co-decision procedure, making the European Parliament in large measure a partner with the Council of Ministers in legislating in certain fields. The treaty extended the existing economic community to co-operation in foreign policy, military and criminal justice. Further strengthening of EU institutions took place with the Amsterdam (1999), Nice (2003) and Lisbon (2009) treaties, the Lisbon Treaty giving the EU a consolidated legal personality, strengthening the institutions of the Union (the Council of Ministers was given power to decide policy by qualified majority instead of unanimity in over forty policy areas) and gave legal recognition to the Charter of Fundamental Rights.

The EC Commission was not only a law-initiating body, but was also responsible for enforcing treaty obligations. It could bring action against a member state if it believed it was in violation of treaty obligations.

Furthermore, law promulgated by the EC was to have effect in the UK without requiring the consent of Parliament. This was provided by section 2(2) of the 1972 act, giving the force of law in the UK to 'rights, powers, liabilities, obligations, and restrictions from time to time created or arising by or under the Treaties'. In effect, therefore, Parliament's assent was given in advance. As the government's 1967 White Paper on membership noted, this was something for which there was no precedent.

Second, it created a new juridical dimension. Membership brought into being a new body of law. Under the 1972 act, questions of law were to be decided by the European Court of Justice (ECJ) or in accordance with decisions of that court. All UK courts were required to take judicial notice of decisions of the European court.

For UK courts, it was not just a case of the courts interpreting the 1972 act, but also EC law that was promulgated under the treaties. The ECJ, now the Court of Justice of the European Union (CJEU), held that laws made under the treaties were independent sources of law. In the *Costa* case in 1964, it asserted that they could not, because of their special and original nature, be overridden by domestic law without depriving it of its character as Community law and calling into question its legal base. 'This case thus unequivocally declared the supremacy of Community – and now EU – law over inconsistent domestic law, including in particular domestic law introduced after accession.'[4]

This supremacy was thus established in the jurisprudence of the ECJ by the time of the UK's membership. As Lord Bridges expressed it in the *Factortame (No. 2)* case in 1991, 'whatever limitation of its sovereignty Parliament accepted when it enacted the European Communities Act 1972 was entirely voluntary. Under the terms of the act of 1972 it has always been clear that it was the duty of the UK court, when delivering final judgment, to override any rule of national law found to be in conflict with any directly enforceable rule of Community law'.[5] Similarly, he noted if the ECJ identified areas of UK law which had failed to implement council directives, Parliament had accepted the obligation to make prompt amendment.

The courts sought to minimise conflict through what Craig termed the technique of avoidance, 'which meant that if a case could be resolved without having to confront the sovereignty issue then this would be the preferred judicial choice'.[6] UK law was construed insofar as possible to render it compatible with EC law. However, in some landmark cases in the 1990s, notably *Factortame* and the *EOC* cases, avoidance was not possible. In the *Factortame* cases, the ECJ held that British courts had the power of injunction and could suspend the application of acts of Parliament that appeared in breach of EU law until a final determination was made. In *R. v. Secretary of State for Employment ex p. the Equal Opportunities Commission*, the House of Lords held certain provisions of the 1978 Employment Protection (Consolidation) Act to be unlawful.[7] In response to the *EOC* case, *The Times* declared that the country may have acquired 'a constitutional court'.[8]

In the *Factortame* case, Lord Bridge sought in effect to square the constitutional circle. UK law that was held by the courts to be in conflict with EC law could be struck down, but the courts could only exercise such power because they were authorised to do so by the provisions of the European Communities Act enacted by Parliament.

However, there remained a fundamental constitutional conundrum. What would happen if Parliament enacted legislation expressly contrary to the UK's obligations? In practice, as Birkinshaw noted, 'It is difficult to envisage circumstances in which this would occur unless the will to remain in the Community had ceased to exist in UK government and Parliament'.[9] The prevailing legal wisdom was expressed in 1979 by the master of the rolls, Lord Denning. If Parliament passed an act repudiating a treaty provision in express terms 'then I should have thought that it would be the duty of our courts to follow the statute of our Parliament'.[10] The courts would thus comply with the wishes of Parliament, but in so doing would render the UK in breach of its obligations under the treaties. The only way in which the UK could extract itself from this situation would be to legislate to withdraw from membership of the EU. But the same problem would remain as, until the Lisbon Treaty, there was no provision to withdraw from the Union. Membership was in perpetuity.

The enactment of the Lisbon Treaty provided in effect an escape clause. The treaty inserted article 50 of the Treaty on European Union enabling a nation to withdraw from membership. There was no evidence to suggest that a member state would likely avail itself of the provision.

From the perspective of the Westminster system, then, membership created new layers of decision-making, political and judicial, that stood above the institutions at the heart of the UK system of government. There was the potential for conflict on specific issues, the EC/EU enacting laws not supported by the UK government and Parliament and the courts striking down provisions of UK law in conflict with European law. In the longer run, there was possibility of the doctrine of parliamentary sovereignty atrophying by virtue of the European treaties taking on the form of the equivalent of a 'written' constitution for the United Kingdom. Indeed, it was argued (though not accepted) in the *Thorburn* case (see Chapter 2) that this had in effect already happened, with the 1972 act effectively serving as a Trojan horse, enabling EU law to become entrenched. 'On this view, EU law was thus capable of having effect in and over domestic law *by virtue of EU law itself*, once the ECA had operated to allow it in.'[11]

The potential for conflict was enhanced by the nature of the Westminster system of government, both the fact of it and adherence to it, and the distinctive features of British history.[12] There was a tension inherent in the UK's membership in that those driving change in the EU adopted a neo-functionalist approach. They saw 'ever closer union' – a goal since the signing of the Treaty of Rome – as a product of societal forces and with integration in one area leading to pressure for integration in others.[13] The stance of British government was more one of intergovernmentalism, seeing the EU as built on co-operation between nation states operating in their national interests.[14] Whereas the former tended to see decision-making as top-down (EU institutions), the latter saw it more as bottom-up (the member states). Succeeding treaties and some decisions of the European court fuelled a sceptical approach to membership by many in the UK, including leading politicians. Margaret Thatcher's Bruges speech brought the tension notably onto the political agenda.

Parliament adapted to EC/EU membership in terms of scrutinising and seeking to influence decision-making in the EC institutions. Each House developed a detailed, committee-based scrutiny process.[15] However, the broader issue of membership remained politically contentious. The more the EU moved towards greater integration, the more critics in the UK pressed for reform. The European Communities (Amendment) Bill giving effect to the Maastricht Treaty badly divided the Conservative Party. The bill also gave rise to a legal challenge.

The challenge, led by Tory peer Lord Rees-Mogg, was on three grounds, one of which was that the queen had no lawful prerogative to transfer her powers in relation to foreign and security policy to the EC as prerogative powers could not be transferred to another body. Lord Rees-Mogg claimed that it was 'the most important constitutional issue to be faced by the courts in 300 years'. The fact of the challenge was raised in the House of Commons as a potential breach of privilege, given that the bill had not yet been passed by Parliament. The Speaker, Betty Boothroyd, ruled that it was not a breach, but nonetheless reminded the courts of the Bill of Rights 1689 stating that the proceedings of Parliament could not be challenged by the courts. In the high court, Lord Justice Lloyd said there was nothing to suggest that in bringing the proceedings the applicant had trespassed on the privileges of Parliament. The court nonetheless found against Lord Rees-Mogg on all three grounds. The treaty establishing a common foreign and security policy was an intergovernmental agreement that could have no effect on domestic law. The act could not be read as a transfer of prerogative powers, but as an exercise of those powers.[16]

Passage of the Maastricht Bill did not still controversy.[17] The Conservative Party was badly divided over the issue of joining a single European currency. When Labour was returned to power in 1997, it committed to holding a referendum should it decide that the UK should join the single currency. Eurosceptic MPs pressed for a referendum on the Lisbon Treaty, but were rebuffed. After David Cameron became prime minister in 2010, he achieved passage of the European Union Act 2011, which provided that any further transfers of power to EU institutions at the expense of national sovereignty, or UK government support for any further amendment in the EU treaties, had first to be approved by an act of Parliament and a referendum (Chapter 5). The nature and extent of Conservative divisions also led him to reversing his stance on having a referendum on continued membership of the EU.[18] The Conservative Party went into the 2015 general election with a manifesto commitment to hold an in/out referendum on membership before the end of 2017 and to honour the outcome, whatever the result.

The UK's membership of the EU has been likened to a marriage. It was one of convenience, joining two suitors from notably different cultures. It was troubled from the beginning, even if the UK dutifully fulfilled its domestic chores.[19] In the end, one side opted for a divorce, made possible by a change in the law. As happens with some divorces, there was an acrimonious dispute over apportioning the assets.

The challenges of withdrawal

The UK was always playing catch-up in terms of understanding the consequences of succeeding treaties. The decision to exit the

EU, following the 2016 referendum in which a majority voted to leave (see Chapter 5), also created novel constitutional challenges. They comprised not only the consequences of withdrawal, but also the process of withdrawal, a unique set of circumstances creating a threat to the fundamental relationship between Parliament and the executive that had existed, or rather was confirmed, by the glorious revolution of 1688. The period witnessed a struggle for control of policy on a scale unknown in modern British history.

In seeking to implement withdrawal from the EU, the government was not only having to negotiate bilaterally (government–European Union), but also consider what was acceptable to other political actors, especially the House of Commons. It was constrained by the courts, by the electors and by Parliament.

The courts. The government announced in 2016 its intention to use prerogative powers to give notification of withdrawal. This led to a legal challenge on the grounds that it required parliamentary approval as rights previously granted by Parliament could only be withdrawn by Parliament. The high court, in *Miller*, upheld the challenge, and on appeal the decision was confirmed by the supreme court.[20] The case proved highly controversial, supporters of Brexit viewing it as an attempt by opponents of withdrawal to thwart the UK leaving the EU. One national newspaper branded the three high court judges who heard the case as 'enemies of the people'.

In consequence of the judgment in *Miller*, the government sought, and achieved passage of, the EU (Notification of Withdrawal) Bill. Parliament thus gave statutory authority to the first step necessary for withdrawal. (There was a subsequent dispute over whether, having given notification, a member state could withdraw it, a matter on which the Treaty on European Union is silent.) Once enacted, the government gave notification of withdrawal and the two-year clock for completion of withdrawal began to tick. The courts – in Scotland, Northern Ireland and England – also became further embroiled in controversy because of the proposed lengthy prorogation of Parliament in 2019, resulting, as we shall see, in a high-profile case before the supreme court. Its significance was such as to result in eleven justices sitting to hear the case and with live television broadcasting of the hearings.

The people. The government's hands were tied by the result of the 2016 referendum. However, they were further tied in 2017 when Prime Minister Theresa May sought, and achieved the agreement of the House of Commons, under the Fixed-Term Parliaments Act (Chapter 8), to an early general election. Instead of giving her, as she hoped, a large Conservative majority to strengthen her negotiating hand, it produced a hung Parliament, the Conservatives having to reach a deal with the Northern Ireland Democratic Unionist Party (DUP), with ten members, in order to command a majority. Although both main parties in their election manifestos were committed to giving effect to the referendum result, the configuration of views of the MPs returned did not guarantee a majority for a specific deal.

Parliament. In preparation for withdrawal, the European Union (Withdrawal) Act 2018 was enacted, providing for the repeal of the 1972 EC Act on 'exit day', but with EU law being retained as part of UK law until a determination was made as to whether to repeal, amend or retain it. The act thus provided for a new category of law, 'retained EU law'. Identifying 'European' law covered by the act was a major challenge, not least given the several forms in which it had been given effect in UK law.

More significantly in terms of achieving agreement on a deal, pressure from MPs, led by Conservative MP Dominic Grieve, resulted – after defeats for the government in both Houses – in ministers agreeing an amendment requiring that before a withdrawal agreement could be ratified, it had to be agreed by a motion of the Commons and an act passed which contains provision 'for the implementation of the withdrawal agreement'. It also contained provision for what the government must do in the event of the motion not being carried.

The government, having entered into negotiations with the EU, produced a withdrawal agreement in November 2018, which it then laid before Parliament. A business motion, moved by Grieve, was carried, which ensured that if a deal was rejected and the government came up with an alternative, the motion providing for that could be subject to amendment.

The vote on the withdrawal agreement was initially postponed when the government feared it would lose and took place eventually on 15 January 2019. It was opposed by all the opposition parties as well as by 118 Conservatives. It was defeated by 432 votes to 202, the biggest defeat for a government in political history. The result led to the leader of the opposition, Jeremy Corbyn, tabling a motion of no confidence in the government, but this was defeated by 325 votes to 306.

There then ensued a tussle between government and the House to find agreement on how to proceed. The result was a failure to approve the withdrawal agreement or to support alternatives. The agreement was put to the House on two further occasions and rejected, on 12 March, by 391 votes to 242 and on 29 March by 344 to 286.

Various amendments were tabled to motions that the government was required to put, pursuant to the 2018 act, but most were rejected. On 29 January, seven amendments were voted on and two were passed: one calling for a renegotiation of the Northern Ireland backstop and the other expressing a desire to avoid a no-deal Brexit. On 14 February, all amendments to a government motion noting ongoing discussions were defeated, as was the motion itself. On 27 February, two amendments were carried, one seeking a joint UK–EU commitment to citizens' rights (carried without a vote) and one stipulating the timetable for a second vote on the agreement (passed by 520 votes to 20). Under the terms of the latter, the government tabled a motion rejecting a no-deal

Brexit. An amendment, rejecting no deal in all circumstances, was carried (by 312 votes to 308); an amendment for a 'managed no-deal Brexit' was rejected (by 374 to 164). In the light of the rejection of the agreement, the government moved a motion, which was agreed, authorising the government to seek an extension of the deadline to 30 June, if the agreement had not been approved by 20 March.

On 25 March, the House agreed an amendment moved by Conservative MP Sir Oliver Letwin for a series of indicative votes and two days later the House voted on eight options, including no deal, revocation of the notification under article 50, and a referendum on the withdrawal agreement. The votes were notable for two reasons. One was that all eight took place simultaneously, using ballot papers. The other was that all eight were voted down. On 1 April, four more indicative votes were held. Again, all were rejected, albeit that supporting membership of a customs union only by 276 votes to 273. The House was against a no-deal Brexit, but it had not voted for an alternative deal. It had not authorised the withdrawal agreement, but it rejected another referendum as well as revocation of the decision to leave.

There was then a move for MPs to take control of the order paper and to pass a bill that would provide for the Commons to decide the date of the extension sought under article 50(3) of the Treaty on European Union. The business motion, moved by Letwin, suspended standing orders so that government business did not have precedence that day and providing that all stages of the bill could be taken in one day. The motion was carried by 312 votes to 311. The European Union (Withdrawal) (No. 5) Bill, sponsored by Labour MP Yvette Cooper and Letwin, was then considered and passed by both Houses. It achieved its second reading by 315 votes to 310.

Theresa May considered bringing the withdrawal agreement back for a fourth vote, but, given the opposition to it and pressure from her own MPs, she resigned. Former foreign secretary Boris

Johnson was elected as party leader to succeed her. He took up office in July 2019 and the following month caused political controversy by seeking prorogation of Parliament from mid-September to mid-October. This was viewed by opponents of Brexit, or leaving the EU without a deal, as an attempt to limit the opportunity for Parliament to debate and constrain the government in preparing to leave the EU by the deadline of 31 October. They took the issue to the courts on the grounds that the prime minister had misled the queen in stating the reasons for seeking prorogation. The case, as we shall see (Chapter 6), raised fundamental constitutional issues, not least the relationship of the courts to the executive and Parliament.

Prior to prorogation, there was essentially a repeat of what Boris Johnson's predecessor had experienced. The House of Commons passed a business motion to take control of the timetable and enable the European Union Withdrawal (No. 6) Bill to be considered and passed. The bill required the prime minister to seek an extension beyond the 31 October deadline for withdrawal, unless the House had agreed a withdrawal agreement or voted for the UK to leave without a deal. The bill passed both Houses and reached the statute book shortly before both Houses were prorogued.

There was, though, movement when the prime minister achieved agreement with the EU on a revised withdrawal agreement, one that most Tory MPs were prepared to support. When the bill to give effect to it, the European Union (Withdrawal Agreement) Bill, was brought before the Commons for second reading on 22 October, it was passed by a majority of 30 (329 votes to 299).[21] However, a timetable motion to ensure the bill was rushed through its remaining stages before 31 October, which would have enabled the UK to leave the EU on that date, was defeated, by 322 votes to 308.[22] In light of the failure to get the bill through by the deadline to which he had committed himself, the prime minister did comply with the provisions of the European Union Withdrawal

(No. 2) Act and write formally to request an extension of negotiations, which was agreed.

Having failed to meet the 31 October deadline, Boris Johnson opted to seek an early general election. He failed on three occasions to get the requisite majority to pass a motion for an early general election under section 2 of the Fixed-Term Parliaments Act (see Chapter 8). However, he was eventually successful, on 29 October, in achieving passage of a bill, which required only a simple majority to pass, stipulating that there would be a general election on 12 December. The 2017–19 Parliament was dissolved at the start of 6 November. In the election, the Conservatives achieved an overall majority of 80 and, on 20 December 2019, a modified version of the bill was given a second reading and arrangements made for its passage by the deadline of 31 January.

The attempt to achieve withdrawal from the EU was thus fraught, politically and constitutionally, even more so than had been the case with joining the EU. The debate over withdrawal proved politically divisive, each side (pro- and anti-Brexit) adopting strident tones. Given that the referendum was not formally binding, the debate was not stilled by the vote, but effectively continued. Constitutionally, it created a clash between the government and the House of Commons, not only to determine outcomes, but to control policy. This was unprecedented. It challenged the fundamental accountability at the heart of the Westminster system.[23] As Vernon Bogdanor noted, only the government can make policy. 'The role of parliament is not to govern but to scrutinise those who do. That is especially the case with the treaty making power. Indeed, parliament has not rejected a treaty since 1864. And parliament is in no position to renegotiate a treaty. It has never in modern times sought to do so.'[24]

The return of a majority Conservative government in December 2019 both brought to an end an exceptional period in British constitutional history and made possible the United Kingdom's withdrawal from the European Union.

Conclusion

The UK's membership of the EC/EU created a novel constitutional situation, one to which it took time for the political system to adapt and in a context where membership was contested. However, the decision to withdraw, in terms of the mechanism employed, and the process of seeking to extract the UK from membership, created novel constitutional conditions that undermined the constitutional edifice of the UK. Independent of the issue of withdrawal, the dispute over the process led to criticism of the crown (agreeing to prorogation), Parliament and the uncodified constitution. Powers were employed that, within the existing constitution, were valid, but used for novel purposes. The events led to claims of a constitutional crisis.[25] This was contested on grounds that the constitutional order had not broken down.[26] Even so, it created constitutional tremors that had not been felt since the early twentieth century over Irish home rule.

Notes

1   Norton 1975: 395–8; Kitzinger 1973: appendix 1.
2   Norton 1978b: 64–82.
3   Thatcher 1988.
4   Bradley *et al.* 2015: 121.
5   [1991] 1 AC 603; Bradley *et al.* 2015: 135.
6   Craig 2018: 113.
7   See Maxwell 1999: 197–211.
8   *The Times*, 5 March 1994, cited in Maxwell 1999: 197.
9   Birkinshaw 2003: 175.
10 Elliott 2018: 227.
11 Elliott 2018: 228.
12 See King 1977: 2–7; McConalogue 2020.
13 Jensen 2003: 80–92.
14 Cini 2003: 93–108.
15 Norton 1996a: 92–109; Norton 2013c: 151–66.
16 [1993] England and Wales High Court of Justice (EWHC) Admin 4.
17 Seldon 1997: 720–7; Norton 1998: 89–93.
18 Norton 2015b: 483–5.

19 Norton 2012d: 252–66.
20 See Elliott *et al.* 2018: 1–38.
21 *HC Deb.* 22 October 2019, cols. 917–20.
22 *HC Deb.* 29 October 2019, cols. 923–6.
23 Norton 2019a.
24 *Guardian*, 29 August 2019.
25 See e.g. Grayling 2017.
26 Ekins and Gee 2018: 255.

Chapter 5

Parliament and referendums: direct or representative democracy?

Referendums are ballots in which electors are asked not to elect, but to pass judgment on a single question or, less usually, set of questions. Their use is frequent in some nations – the world leader is Switzerland, where they are held frequently – and infrequent or impermissible in others.[1] In the United States, they are employed in some states, but a nation-wide referendum is not possible under the US constitution. An attempt in the 1930s to amend the constitution, to provide for one on the issue of war (the Ludlow amendment), failed in the House of Representatives.

In the United Kingdom, their use at anything other than at local level was, until the 1970s, unknown, but variously advocated. Their advocacy developed at the end of the nineteenth century and at the beginning of the twentieth. They have moved from being devices unknown to the constitution, to being used on occasion, as well as promised on others, to determine particular contested issues of constitutional importance. Their use is sanctioned on each occasion by Parliament. They are within the gift of Parliament, but their very use raises fundamental issues about democracy, and especially accountability, within the political system. They are not obviously compatible with the Westminster system of government.

Advocacy and use

The concept of referring an issue to the people was developed in the late 1860s by the Conservative leader in the House of Lords, the 3rd Marquess of Salisbury, but what was entailed was not a referendum as such, but rather triggering a general election on a specific issue. If the House of Commons passed a measure on which the views of the country were not clear, the House of Lords was entitled to 'insist that the nation shall be consulted'.[2] Advocacy in this form reflected political goals, the Conservatives, enjoying a majority in the upper house, wanting to force elections on Liberal policies to which they objected.

The first attempt to provide for a referendum was made in 1896 by a Liberal MP, Robert Wallace. He moved a motion stating that it was desirable to introduce the principle of an initiative or referendum, 'with the view of more fully securing the direct and continuous control of the Legislature by the people'. He cited the experience of Switzerland and argued that the people were as good judges as anyone of the main object of the law.[3] The speech was a lone one and appears to have made no impression on the House.

What brought the issue on to the political agenda was the intense conflict over Irish home rule that dominated British politics in the late nineteenth and early twentieth centuries. Opponents saw a referendum as a means of preventing home rule being implemented through legislation. The principal proponent of the referendum was none other than A. V. Dicey.[4] He saw it as a 'people's veto'. Opposition to home rule influenced stances on reform of the House of Lords in the constitutional crisis generated by the Lords' rejection of the Liberal government's budget in 1909.[5] Where people stood on reform was shaped by their stance on home rule: supporters wanted to preserve the existing House as a means of blocking a home rule bill; opponents saw it as an impediment. When the Lords' powers to veto legislation was restricted by the Parliament Act 1911, the referendum became the favoured means of blocking change. It was not confined to home rule, but offered as a potential means of resolving the constitutional crisis over the Lords in 1910 and the issue of tariff reform, the latter included in the Conservative 1910 election manifesto.[6] The Conservatives used their majority in the Lords to include provision in the Parliament Bill for referendums on home rule and other constitutional issues. The Commons rejected the provision. It constituted the first time the two Houses had voted on the issue.

The Bryce conference on the reform of the second chamber, which reported in 1918, also considered the use of referendums, but rejected their use on several grounds. A referendum 'could not be confined to the cases for which it was in this instance proposed'. Furthermore, 'it might tend to lower the authority and dignity of Parliament, and … was unsuited to the conditions of a large country, and especially of the United Kingdom, for different parts of which different legislation is sometimes required'.[7]

Thereafter, the use of a referendum was proposed for certain issues, but by individual politicians rather than by parties. The Conservative commitment to one on tariff reform was dropped after Bonar Law became party leader. Some opponents of female suffrage, including leading politicians such as Winston Churchill and later Lord Curzon, proposed one on the issue. Conservative leader Stanley Baldwin in 1930 advocated one on protection – essentially picking up where Balfour had left off on tariff reform – and in 1945 Winston Churchill considered having one to decide whether the parties should continue in coalition until the war with Japan was completed.

There are two generalisations that can be drawn about advocacy of referendums during this period. The first is that their proponents tended to be Conservative politicians. For them, referendums were a limiting device, a double-lock to prevent radical constitutional change. They failed, though, to make headway, essentially for two reasons. One was that for much of the century, the Conservatives were in government and so saw no need to place a restraint on government policies. The other was that what was a conservative device was not necessarily a Conservative one. Referendums challenged the Westminster model of government, raising, as we shall see, fundamental issues of accountability. The Labour Party was, as we have noted (Chapter 1), averse to constitutional change that could limit a Labour government in achieving its radical social goals. In 1945, Labour leader Clement Attlee gave short shrift to Churchill's call for one. The Liberals showed little interest, being wary of what could be seen as a device by which a majority could discriminate against a minority.

The other generalisation is that referendums were advocated at times of major constitutional conflict. They were seen as a means to an end and not as ends in themselves. It was not a case of advocating, as a matter of principle, consulting the people on a particular category of issues, such as changes to the tenets of the constitution. Rather, it was a case of consulting the people on a specific issue which proponents considered of fundamental importance and in conditions where they thought voters may produce an outcome not achievable through Parliament. The UK royal commission on the constitution, which reported in 1973, noted that popular interest in a referendum on the UK's entry into the European Communities appeared to be widespread. However, it noted, it 'arose out of a particular and transient situation and against the background of referenda [*sic*] being held in other countries faced with the same decision. It did not appear to be part of a general and continuous demand for referenda on all important issues'.[8]

The combination of Conservative administrations and an absence of major constitutional conflict for most of the century explains why advocacy of referendums was not a notable, and certainly not a consistent, feature of political debate. Indeed, discussion in parliamentary debates was noteworthy for its rarity. In 1967, Conservative MP Harold Gurden sought to introduce a private member's ten-minute rule bill to provide 'for a referendum to be held with a general election', with the referendum on issues selected by Parliament, but limited in number. 'My supporters and I have immediately in mind as issues for a referendum such particularly contentious items as the reintroduction of corporal punishment and capital punishment', he said. 'Recent changes in the law relating to homosexuality and to abortion will be in people's minds at the moment.'[9] The people, he contended, should have their say on issues on which parties had not sought a mandate. Labour MP Denis Coe put the case against, partly on practical grounds (timing, selection of topics, turnout), but also on principle. It would 'work away from our system of representative government on which the whole of our democracy rests. In a system of government such as ours, the centre of democracy must rest with this Chamber'.[10] On a voice vote, Gurden was denied leave to bring in his bill. Debate had occupied a total of fifteen minutes.

Six years later, Parliament legislated for a referendum in Northern Ireland on the question of whether the people in Northern Ireland wished it to remain in the UK. Nearly 600,000 voted to remain, against just over 6,000 voting to leave. However, its holding was seen as specific to the situation in Northern Ireland and not viewed as creating a precedent for others. It confirmed what was known rather than resolving a contentious issue where the outcome was unknown.

The issue of using the referendum may thus have languished – the UK had not employed one on a kingdom-wide basis and no significant figures, or parties, were pressing for one – had it not been for conflict again over a contentious constitutional issue. Whereas Irish home rule had formed the fault line of British politics in the late nineteenth and early twentieth centuries, so the issue of European integration formed the fault line in the years after 1945, culminating in notable conflict in the late twentieth and early twenty-first centuries.

The principal target of demands for a referendum was the UK's joining of the EC. As we have seen (Chapter 4), membership raised important constitutional issues. Debate over the merits of joining also gave rise to demands for membership to be put to a referendum. During passage of the European Communities Bill in 1972, Conservative backbencher Neil Marten, a leading opponent of membership, moved an amendment providing that the act would not take effect until a consultative advisory referendum had been held.

The amendment divided not only the parties, but also members within each. Having previously opposed referendums, the opposition under Harold Wilson supported the amendment, arguing that the government had no mandate for the measure. The chancellor of the duchy of Lancaster, Geoffrey Rippon, argued that it would add nothing to understanding the issues involved, and would weaken public confidence in the ability and authority of its elected representatives. The amendment was defeated by 284 votes to 235. More than fifty Labour MPs abstained from voting. Three, including deputy leader Roy Jenkins, resigned from the front bench over the issue. On the government side, twenty-two Tory MPs voted for the amendment and about nine abstained.[11]

However, what transformed the situation was the return of a Labour government to office in 1974. The UK was already a member of the EC. Prime Minister Harold Wilson headed a party badly divided over Britain's membership. He decided that a referendum on membership would be a means of holding it together. Parliament enacted legislation for the referendum. Wilson engaged in negotiations with the EC to make some adjustment to the terms of membership and the question put in the referendum was whether the UK should remain a member of the EC on the basis of renegotiated terms. In the event, with both main parties and most of the British press supporting staying in the EC, there was an overwhelming 'yes' vote, with 17.3 million voting to remain and 8.4 million voting to leave.[12] The vote was seen to still debate on membership, at least for the foreseeable future. The vote may have maintained the status quo in terms of EC membership, thus avoiding a constitutional upheaval, but the use of a UK-wide referendum set a precedent. Although it was to be another thirty-six years before another UK-wide referendum was held, the government was willing to deploy referendums in different parts of the UK.

The Labour government introduced legislation in 1978 to provide for referendums on devolution in Scotland and Wales. The House of Commons passed amendments, against the wishes of ministers, stipulating that if 40 per cent of those entitled to vote failed to vote 'yes' then orders giving effect to the act would be repealed. In Scotland, although there was a majority 'yes' vote, it failed to meet the 40 per cent threshold. In Wales, there was a decisive 'no' vote. As a result, powers were not devolved to either nation.

When Labour was returned to office in 1997, it again legislated for referendums in Scotland and Wales, and also – consequent to the Good Friday Agreement – in Northern Ireland. Each referendum resulted in a yes vote, albeit narrowly in the case of Wales. There was also some element of devolution to London, also based on a referendum in the capital. These referendums not only provided for constitutional change to the governmental structure of the United Kingdom, but also essentially confirmed referendums as part of the nation's constitutional architecture. The government not only achieved passage of legislation for referendums, it also committed to holding one should it decide to join a single European currency.

As we have noted (Chapter 1), further referendums followed under governments after 2010, the two partners to the coalition government in 2010 agreeing to legislate for a UK-wide referendum on the use of the alternative vote – held in 2011 – and to the Scottish government holding one in 2014 on Scotland becoming an independent state. (There was also a referendum in Wales in 2011 on giving more powers to the National Assembly for Wales, triggered under the provisions of the Government of Wales Act

2006.) The Conservative government elected in 2015 implemented an election pledge to legislate for a UK-wide in/out referendum on membership of the EU.

Governments pursue referendums primarily for tactical reasons and normally seek parliamentary approval when they believe that they are likely to get the outcomes they want – and generally do.[13] The government in 2016 believed that there would be a vote to remain – Prime Minister David Cameron apparently seeing it as a rerun of what happened in 1975 – and was somewhat blindsided when there was a no vote, something for which it had made no preparation. The narrow majority in the referendum, the government's unpreparedness for the outcome, and a somewhat indecisive outcome when new prime minister Theresa May achieved the Commons' agreement to a general election in 2017, created conditions, as we have seen (Chapter 4), that were constitutionally novel.

The controversy over implementing Brexit appeared to dampen enthusiasm for referendums, but it was too late to remove them as mechanisms to be employed to resolve contentious political issues or to confirm major changes in the devolution settlement. Provisions for referendums to be used in specified circumstances were embodied in a number of statutes (Government of Wales Act 2006, European Union Act 2011, Scotland Act 2016, Government of Wales Act 2017). They are thus formally acknowledged and in certain circumstances also likely to be politically unavoidable. For some, they constitute valuable democratic tools. For others, a necessary (or unnecessary, but unavoidable) evil.

People or Parliament?

The key argument of principle is one of direct democracy versus representative democracy. The motivation for holding a referendum may be one of political expediency – not least holding together a party (as with the 1975 and 2016 referendums) or a coalition (the

2011 referendum) – but the justification is one of enabling voters to determine the outcome on a key issue of public policy.

The principal argument advanced for referendums is that advanced by Vernon Bogdanor, namely that they supplement, rather than challenge, representative government by seeking the approval of the people.[14] Various witnesses to the Lords' constitution committee, in its inquiry into referendums, viewed them as means for countering public distrust in the political system. They could help counteract the sense of cynicism and powerless among voters. The government view at the time was that referendums could provide the government with a mandate to undertake change and provide Parliament with an indication of public opinion on a given issue. They could serve to legitimise change.[15]

The fact that referendums are advisory means that the hands of Parliament are not formally tied. It could choose not to act in line with the outcome. Even if a referendum is made binding, it is made so by an act of Parliament. Parliament could choose subsequently to amend it or pass a new act overturning it.

In the context of the UK, opposition has been on grounds of maintaining parliamentary sovereignty. The use of referendums can be seen as a fundamental challenge to that sovereignty. Charles McIlwain quoted an American who queried whether parliamentary sovereignty in any form 'can long survive the triumph of democracy … When the Referendum really comes, the sovereign Parliament must go'.[16]

A referendum in practice represents Parliament handing decision-making to the people. This undermines the role of Parliament as a deliberative body. It also raises fundamental issues of accountability.

Parliament is a highly institutionalised legislature, with well-established processes for considering measures of public policy. The merits and practical problems can be debated at different stages, with the rules providing for both sides to be heard. Evidence can be processed through committees and assessed in debate.

Although both Houses vote on the principle of a measure, they get to consider amendments. With a referendum, there is usually a single vote on a binary choice. It is the equivalent of the electors voting on the second reading of a bill (yes or no), but without the opportunity to address options and amendments. Although attempts have been made to provide for each side of the argument in a referendum debate to have a fair hearing, with one side not having resources disproportionate to another, legislating for that has proved problematic.

Perhaps most important is the issue of accountability. Under the Westminster model, as we have seen, electors choose representatives to act on their behalf. A government is formed usually by the majority party in the House of Commons and it stands before electors at the next general election. Furthermore it stands on a particular platform. It therefore has a mandate to act. It does not require an additional one. When a referendum was pushed for on EC membership in 1972, the Solicitor-General, Sir Geoffrey Howe, took the view that 'The electorate *had* endorsed the principle of membership [in the 1970 general election]. The final crucial stage could properly be entrusted to Parliament itself'.[17] Electors can judge the government's performance and decide at the next election whether to continue its mandate or turn it out of office. The government is thus accountable to electors for what it has done. With referendums, there is no accountability. Electors cannot hold themselves to account for the outcome of a referendum.

Once a referendum has been held, it falls to Parliament to give effect to the outcome. Parliament formally could decide not to act on the outcome. It could make them binding by legislating for a referendum and including provision to give effect to the outcome. That happened in the case of the 2011 referendum on the electoral system. Had there been a 'yes' vote, the alternative vote (AV) would have been introduced for parliamentary elections. The government also achieved passage in 2011 of the European Union

Act, which provided that a transfer of power to EU institutions at the expense of national sovereignty, or any UK government support for amendments to EU treaties, had to be approved by act of Parliament and a referendum. The referendum would be binding in that the government was barred from ratifying a treaty if the referendum had failed to approve it. The two UK-wide referendums on membership of the EC/EU were not made binding, generating in the wake of the 2016 referendum intense debate over whether Parliament should decline to give effect to the result, given the narrowness of the majority.

There is the allied problem for Parliament in that referendums reveal definitively how people voted, but not why they voted as they did. Did those voting 'no' in the 2014 independence referendum in Scotland favour more devolution, as party leaders assumed they did, or less? Survey evidence suggests several different reasons for voting against independence; that of favouring more devolution hardly registered.[18] Surveys also indicate that, although the desire for decisions to be taken at UK rather than EU level was a significant influence in voting 'leave' in the 2016 referendum,[19] the vote to leave 'reflected a complex, cross-cutting mix of calculations, emotions and cues'.[20] As Evans and Menon observed, the binary choice that was offered to electors 'contained at least four discrete options' (remain, the 'Norway', 'Canada' and World Trade Organization options).[21] Governments thus know how electors voted, but lack definitive evidence as to their reasons for doing so. This poses challenges in seeking to implement the outcomes.

There is thus a clash between the two sovereignties identified by Dicey. Parliament enjoys legal sovereignty, the electors enjoy political sovereignty. So long as parliamentarians are chosen by voters and given discretion in between elections to exercise their legal sovereignty, there is usually no problem. The political system is premised on that relationship. The use of referendums introduces a problem in that, in practice if not formally, it denies the discretion afforded Parliament.

Margaret Thatcher, in her first major speech as leader of the opposition in 1975, advanced the key constitutional objections. She noted that the lord president of the council had argued that holding a referendum did not derogate from the principle of parliamentary sovereignty, but that he had said that it would give the final say to the British people. 'That shows our constitutional difficulty in discussing this subject and in taking decisions before we have thought about them properly and considered all the consequences.'[22] On representative democracy, Parliament comprised a body in which different sides of an argument could be considered, and minorities protected. For MPs, it would, as a number argued in the same debate, be an abdication of their responsibilities. As Labour MP John Macintosh expressed it, 'The fundamental assumption behind the referendum is that this House does not adequately represent the feelings of the country'.[23]

Consequences

Referendums create a conundrum for Parliament. By legislating, they hand decision-making in effect to voters. This may be popular, but it undermines the standing of the institution. Parliament agrees to a referendum usually because the governing party or parties are divided on an issue, but by seeking to resolve intra-party differences, it undermines its own legitimacy as the determinant of public policy. Members prioritise loyalty to party over commitment to the institution of which they are members. The more parties are divided, the greater the potential for issues to be referred to a referendum. The more referendums there are, the more people come to expect them.

Harold Wilson told the House of Commons in 1975, 'The circumstances of this referendum are unique'.[24] So long as the circumstances of each are seen as 'unique', there will be no certainty as to when they will be held. Demands will thus be made for referendums on subjects that people deem to be (to them) of fundamental importance, which can only be resolved by a vote of the people. Referendums have been held on constitutional issues, but, as we have seen, Harold Gurden in 1967 envisioned having them on social issues. Margaret Thatcher as Conservative leader thought there may be a case for one on trade union reform.

The constitution committee of the House of Lords in a report on referendums identified 'fundamental constitutional issues' on which, if referendums were to be held, it would be most appropriate to employ them. As it acknowledged, the list was not definitive and it did not think it possible to provide a precise definition of what constituted a fundamental constitutional issue. Those that it listed included proposals 'to abolish either House of Parliament'.[25] The problems it identified were borne out two years later when the government introduced a House of Lords Reform Bill to replace the existing second chamber with a predominantly elected chamber. Opponents argued that the measure amounted to the abolition of the existing House and pressed for a referendum. A joint committee set up by both Houses to consider the bill in draft recommended it be subject to a referendum. The government argued it was not abolishing the second chamber and did not regard it as a fundamental issue falling to be referred to the people.

The conundrum had been identified earlier, in 2000, when the Political Parties, Elections and Referendums Bill was being debated in the House of Lords. Former foreign secretary Lord Owen moved an amendment to provide for referendums on issues of 'first class' constitutional importance. The question was raised as to where precisely the line could be drawn between issues that were of first class importance and those that were second class.

The other problem is that the outcome of a referendum may not serve its core purpose, which is to resolve an issue. This has been exemplified in the UK by the outcomes of the 2014 independence referendum in Scotland and the 2016 UK referendum on membership of the EU. In both cases, those on the losing side did not see the issue as resolved and pressed for a new referendum.

In 2018, an independent commission on referendums advanced proposals to provide a more structured framework for referendums.[26] It advanced an eleven-point checklist. This included questions such as 'Is interest in the subject adequate to ensure a high level of turnout?' 'Are the alternatives clear, or do they need further consideration?' and 'Is a referendum the best way of involving citizens in the decision in question, or might some other means of public consultation serve at least as well, or better?' If the answer to any one of the eleven questions was no, then the referendum, it said, should not be held at that point. Also, when planning a referendum, it identified three other questions to be addressed, including 'What can be done to reduce the risk of polarisation and lasting political divisions after the referendum?' These potential hurdles, if accepted and utilised either as guidelines or as legislative provisions, would limit use of referendums, but not prevent them.

Conclusion

The use of referendums injects a tension within the Westminster system of government. Formally, there is no conflict if Parliament legislates for what is an advisory referendum and is not therefore bound by the result. The people feed in their view and it is then a matter for Parliament to act on it. The political reality is different in that once a referendum is held, those who have voted, at least those in the majority, expect the result to be implemented. Parliament is not bound constitutionally to implement the result. Politically, it is largely unavoidable. The campaigns can be highly divisive, as in Scotland in 2014 and in the UK in 2016, resolving neither the issue for the foreseeable future nor strengthening popular support for political parties[27] nor the body that legislated for them.[28]

Parliament may also tie its hands by providing that the outcome of a referendum will be binding, that is, take effect with Parliament having to legislate. As we have seen, the 2011 referendum was binding in that Parliament had legislated in advance that a 'yes' vote would have led to a new electoral system being introduced. (The Northern Ireland Act 1998 provisions for a referendum may also be seen as binding in that they imposed obligations on ministers in the event of a particular outcome.) The European Union Act 2011 provided electors with a veto. The measure gave the electorate 'the legal right of political veto over the actions of the government and the wishes of Parliament, and may be seen as a vindication of popular sovereignty at the expense of parliamentary sovereignty. Parliament may approve the treaty, but the electorate may not, in which case the will of Parliament must give way to the will of the people'.[29]

Indeed, the period 2016–19 demonstrated what happens when the two concepts of democracy – direct and representative – collide. The 2016 referendum was an exercise in direct democracy. Electors voted in favour of the UK's withdrawal from the EU. The 2017 general election was an exercise in representative democracy. The election produced a House of Commons that could not agree on the terms for withdrawing from the EU (Chapter 4). Electors cannot hold themselves to account for the outcome of a referendum. Neither can they hold to account a transient majority in the House of Commons. The accountability at the heart of the Westminster system was the victim of the collision.

Notes

1 See Butler and Ranney 1994; Qvortrup 2005, 2018a.
2 *Parliamentary Debates* 17 June 1869, col. 84; Norton 2013d: 156.
3 *HC Deb.* 21 February 1896, cols. 873–8.
4 Dicey 1973.
5 Norton 2012c: 444–59.
6 LeMay 1979: 198; Adams 1999: 44.
7 Command Paper 9038; LeMay 1979: 158.
8 Royal Commission on the Constitution 1973: 98.
9 *HC Deb.* 17 July 1967, col. 1450.
10 *HC Deb.* 17 July 1967, col. 1453.

11 Norton 1975: 435–6.

12 Butler and Kitzinger 1976; King 1977.

13 Lijphart 1984: 203; Butler and Ranney 1994: 261; Qvortrup 2018b: 79; see also Constitution Committee, House of Lords 2010a: 16.

14 Bogdanor 1997: 144; 2009: 174.

15 Michael Wills MP; Constitution Committee, House of Lords 2010a: 13.

16 Cited in Pollard 1920: 2.

17 Howe 1994: 67.

18 Henderson 2019: 46–7.

19 McConalogue 2020: 238–9.

20 Clarke *et al.* 2017: 174.

21 Evans and Menon 2017: 93.

22 *HC Deb.* 11 March 1975, col. 305.

23 *HC Deb.* 11 March 1975, col. 336.

24 *HC Deb.* 23 January 1975, cols. 1745–7; see also Bogdanor 2009: 182.

25 Constitution Committee, House of Lords 2010a: 27.

26 Constitution Unit 2018.

27 Evans and Menon 2017: 88–9.

28 Hansard Society 2019.

29 Bradley *et al.* 2015: 140.

Chapter 6

Parliament and the courts: strangers, foes or friends?

Whereas Chapter 2 addressed a hierarchy of principles (parliamentary sovereignty and the rule of law), here we address institutional relationships. The creation of the UK supreme court in 2009, replacing the appellate committee of the House of Lords as the nation's highest court, raised the issue of the relationship between this new distinct body and the other elements of the constitutional system – the executive and Parliament. How has the relationship of the court to each other element changed in recent years? Three models have been developed that provide a framework for analysis.[1] Is the relationship in each case one of *respective autonomy* (each operating independently of the other), *competing authority* (clashing over policy and their capacity to determine outcomes) or what has been termed *democratic dialogue* (operating in comity with one another)?

There has been a confluence of two developments that has affected the relationship of the courts both to Parliament and to the government. One is the changing constitutional landscape. The court has now to deal with matters that were not previously within its scope. The second is the impact of a physical move, the members of the House of Lords appellate committee moving across Parliament Square to occupy a new building and forming the supreme court of the United Kingdom.

These developments have contributed to a changing relationship as the twenty-first century has progressed. In the twentieth century, the relationship of the courts to the other two elements – Parliament and the executive – was one primarily of respective autonomy. Since then, the relationship of the courts to Parliament has moved more to one of democratic dialogue, especially in the wake of the creation of the supreme court. The relationship of the courts to the executive has been more problematic and has exhibited elements of competing authority. The courts and Parliament have on occasion come together to constrain or influence the executive.

Constitutional change

Membership of the European Union, enactment of the Human Rights Act, and devolution have created a new juridical dimension to the constitution. As we have seen (Chapter 4), as a consequence of membership of the EC, now the EU, the senior courts acquired powers to strike down provisions of UK law as incompatible with EU law. This resulted in the courts achieving greater public and political visibility, especially in the 1990s in the *Factortame* and *EOC* cases. However, the controversy in these cases was arguably as nothing compared to the cases arising from the decision for the UK to withdraw from membership of the EU. The high court and supreme court attracted criticism in 2016 for holding in the *Miller* case that notification of withdrawal from the EU under article 50 of the Treaty on European Union could not be undertaken by prerogative powers, but it required the approval of Parliament.

Equally, the courts attracted controversy in September 2019 when the prime minister's request to prorogue Parliament for five weeks was challenged in courts in Scotland, Northern Ireland and England. The challenge was on the grounds that it was employed improperly to prevent Parliament considering the government's plans for the UK's exit from the EU. The supreme court's decision,

holding that the advice to prorogue was unlawful, constituted arguably its most important judgment since it came into being. As we
shall see, the prime minister announced he 'profoundly disagreed'
with the judgment, but nonetheless complied with it.

The Human Rights Act 1998 created a new role for judges in
interpreting rights under the ECHR. In order to ensure that they
were trained in a task that was novel to them, the main provisions
of the act did not come into force until 2000. The number of cases
reaching the senior courts in which declarations of incompatibility
have been made has been small, averaging about two a year, but
some have been controversial, attracting significant criticism from
the media and from ministers.

In 2004, in the *Belmarsh* case, the law lords held that powers in
Part 4 of the Anti-Terrorism, Crime and Security Act 2001 were
disproportionate and discriminatory in applying only to foreign
nationals. Foreign Secretary Jack Straw declared that the judges
were 'simply wrong' and that it was for Parliament, not the courts,
to determine how Britain could be defended from terrorism.[2] The
government did amend the law in light of the judgment, but the
new law also fell foul of the courts.

The courts attracted criticism for adhering too closely to
the 'mirror principle' and following the interpretation of the
European Court on Human Rights (EctHR) at Strasbourg.
Although the senior courts started to follow less closely the mirror
principle, there were judgments of the EctHR that constrained
the UK courts and further fuelled controversy. In *Hirst* v. *UK (No.
2)* in 2005, the Strasbourg court held that the UK's blanket ban
on prisoners being allowed to vote was incompatible with convention rights. In *Smith* v. *Scott* (2007) the law lords duly issued a
declaration of incompatibility. This led the government to prevari-
cate and spend years kicking the issue, as Jack Straw conceded,
'into touch'.[3] The House of Commons also voted overwhelmingly
against giving prisoners a vote. A joint committee of both Houses
of Parliament set up to examine a draft bill on the subject reported

in 2013, recommending prisoners serving twelve months or less be permitted to vote, but the government never issued a substantive response to the report. It was another five years – more than a decade after the original *Hirst* judgment – before a compromise was reached, whereby some prisoners were permitted to vote.

'Since 1998', as Brice Dickson has noted, 'it can plausibly be claimed that even though there is still no written constitution for the whole of the United Kingdom there are written Constitutions for the three devolved parts of the United Kingdom'.[4] The legislation creating elected bodies in Scotland, Wales and Northern Ireland, and subsequent amending acts, resulted in the senior courts serving in effect as constitutional courts for the devolved nations, with power to strike down measures of the devolved legislatures on grounds of being beyond the scope of the devolution legislation. The courts accord the devolved legislatures a margin of appreciation by virtue of the fact that they are elected and therefore, as Lord Hope of Craighead put it in the *Axa* case, 'the judges should intervene, if at all, only in the most exceptional circumstances'. The courts nonetheless are variously called upon to decide devolution issues. There is an overlap with the previous influence, in that most devolution issues coming before the supreme court are brought on grounds of conflict with convention rights. Law officers are also empowered to refer bills before they have received royal assent to the supreme court to determine if they are within scope of the powers vested by the devolution legislation. Some references have been made in respect of measures passed by the National Assembly for Wales. In recognition of its role, the supreme court has held sittings in both Edinburgh and Cardiff.

The impact of space

Instead of being within the Palace of Westminster, the court now sits facing the palace across Parliament Square. On the surface, there has been little change in terms of personnel and powers.

The twelve law lords – the nation's highest judges – moved from the Palace of Westminster to the new supreme court building, what had previously been Middlesex Guildhall. However, physical constructs and location, and how space is used, make a difference to behaviour and outcomes.[5]

Prior to 1941, judicial hearings took place in the chamber of the House of Lords. When the chamber of the House of Commons was destroyed by enemy bombing, the Commons moved into the Lords' chamber and the Lords relocated to the king's robing room. 'After the war the noise of rebuilding work made conditions in the Robing Room so intolerable that it was suggested that, as a purely temporary measure, an Appellate Committee should be appointed so that the Law Lords could hear appeals in one of the upstairs committee rooms where they would not be disturbed by the noise.'[6] The appellate committee became a permanent feature, with judicial hearings taking place in committee rooms in the palace – principally committee room 1 in the House of Lords – though with judgments still delivered in the chamber. The judicial sittings of the chamber were separate from the regular sittings of the House and were attended usually only by the law lords, with barristers in each case stood at the bar of the House.

In the nineteenth century the judicial and legislative roles of the House of Lords became more sharply distinguished. Law lords were appointed to the House as Lords of Appeal in Ordinary under the Appellate Jurisdiction Act 1876 – they became the earliest form of life peers – but could if they wished take part in regular sittings of the House. Over time, their involvement in the chamber declined. Some occasionally spoke, not least on the administration of justice, but generally they abstained from voting and from speaking on matters that may be politically contentious. Two did, though, attract criticism at the start of the twenty-first century by voting on the issue of banning foxhunting.

Although operating as a distinct entity, the law lords were nonetheless visible in the House of Lords. They had offices there – there was a law lords' corridor, initially on the principal floor, but later on the second floor of the palace – and variously dined together in the peers' dining room. After the House established a European Communities, later EU, committee, it became the convention for a law lord to chair sub-committee E, dealing with law and institutions. That entailed chairing meetings of the sub-committee, overseeing the drafting of reports, and speaking to the reports if they were debated in the chamber. It was thus possible for other peers to see them in the palace, including when they contributed to debates, and to have some awareness of what they were doing. They were thus known entities. There was some appreciation of who they were and what they did.

The government in 2005 achieved enactment of the Constitutional Reform Act, creating a supreme court. The government argued that having judgments delivered by 'the House of Lords' was confusing. It believed that the public had difficulty distinguishing the House of Lords in its judicial capacity (the law lords) from the House of Lords in its political capacity (the whole House). Originally, there was no distinction. The House of Lords as a whole exercised the judicial functions of the high court of Parliament, but in time the judicial role came to be fulfilled by legally qualified peers. The separation of the law lords – the Lords of Appeal in Ordinary and other senior judges – from the rest of the House became complete in the nineteenth century.

Once the new building was ready in 2009, the supreme court came into being. Although only a short distance from the Palace of Westminster, there were fears on the part of some commentators and indeed judges that the move could affect how the court was seen. Members of the House of Lords would not have the same appreciation of the role of the court as previously held. Turnover of membership in the Lords as well as in the supreme court would mean that over time each would be a somewhat alien body to the other. There were conflicting views of the effect of this change. One was that the court would be more isolated than before and vulnerable to criticism when reaching decisions that went against the government.[7] The House of Lords would be less likely to act as a buffer between the court and the executive at a time when conflict, because of judgments in human rights or EU law cases, was likely to be greater than before.

The other, contrasting, view was that having a more distinct identity would embolden members of the court and encourage greater independence in developing the court's jurisprudence. The government, in making the case for the creation of the court, claimed that it 'would reflect and enhance the independence of the Judiciary from both the legislature and the executive'.[8]

In practice, the separation has tended to propel both the supreme court and Parliament to seek some measure of dialogue, with some benefit to each, while the relationship of the court to the executive has been more difficult and at times fraught. The changes in the relationship can be seen through examining each of the three models.

Three models

Respective autonomy

The respective autonomy model posits that the courts are, in functional terms, strangers to both Parliament and the executive. The courts have their own role to fulfil and operate independently of the other branches, respecting their roles as they respect the independence and autonomy of the courts. As Lord Nicholls of Birkenhead put it in *Wilson* v. *Secretary of State for Trade and Industry* in 2004, 'Parliament enacts legislation, the courts interpret and apply it'. The physical closeness of senior judges and parliamentarians meant there was little need for formal structures to facilitate dialogue. In addition to the law lords, various other senior judges also sat in the House of Lords. These included the lord chief justice, who sat by virtue of his position, whereas other peers sat who happened to hold judicial office. For a good part of the twentieth century, the House of Commons included some senior barristers who gave up membership to become judges. Thus, for example, Jocelyn Simon gave up his seat in 1962 in order to become president of the probate, divorce and admiralty division of the high court, later becoming a law lord. There was an element of mutual trust, reinforced by the nature of the courts operating in such a way as not to encroach on the activities of government or Parliament. The courts could not strike down acts of Parliament and the power to hold that ministers were acting *ultra vires* or contrary to the common law concept of natural justice was not much in evidence.[9] The courts were seen as somewhat deferential to the state as represented by the executive.

There was a change in the latter half of the twentieth century, with judges demonstrating a greater degree of judicial activism than before, with a growing willingness to review executive actions. A corollary of the growth of the state was a greater involvement of the courts in ensuring ministers stayed within the limits imposed by statute and common law. In the 1960s and succeeding decades, the courts proved active in reviewing the actions of administrative bodies and of ministers. In some notable cases, the courts ruled against such bodies.[10] In *Padfield* v. *Minister of Agriculture, Fisheries and Food* in 1968, the House of Lords held that a minister could not employ discretionary powers if their exercise thwarted the object of the act conferring those powers. The courts no longer took the exercise of ministerial power at face value, but they have proved willing to look at the reasons for the exercise of that power.

This judicial activism preceded the constitutional developments already mentioned, starting with the European Communities Act 1972. There was also a change in the nature of the House of Commons, with fewer senior barristers serving and going on to hold judicial office, a point noted by the lord chief justice, Lord Thomas of Cwmgiedd, in a 2014 lecture.[11] As he later observed in the 2017 Michael Ryle memorial lecture: 'One consequence of this greater separation between Parliament and judiciary has been the risk that the two will have a decreasing understanding of their constitutional roles, ways of working and ways of working with each other.'[12]

The understanding of roles came increasingly to rely on the House of Lords. The relationship of respective autonomy was one understood by the law lords.[13] As Lord Nicholls of Birkenhead put it in the *Wilson* case, 'The House sitting in its judicial capacity is keenly aware, as indeed are all courts, of the importance of the legislature and judiciary discharging their own constitutional roles and not trespassing inadvertently into the other's province'.[14] The *Wilson* case is instructive in that it entailed the House of Lords slapping down the court of appeal for straying too far in examining parliamentary proceedings to determine why Parliament had enacted a particular provision.

Once the government achieved passage of the Constitutional Reform Act, this threw into sharp relief the relationship between Parliament and the judiciary. The act not only removed the law lords from the House, for the period they served as law lords, but similarly also disbarred from membership peers who held judicial office, such as lord chief justice, for the period they held office. The severing of the judges from the House alarmed various senior office holders, including the lord chief justice, who grasped the significance of losing the means by which to raise issues with Parliament. The effect was subsequently encapsulated in Lord Thomas' 2017 lecture:

> Thus, although one of the objectives of the 2005 Act was to make clear the position of the judiciary as a separate and independent branch of the State, 10 years on it has become very clear that a proper method of working between the judiciary, the Executive and Parliament has had to be established … somewhat paradoxically the 2005 Act and the agreements associated with it have not only provided the necessity for working together, but, if observed, provided a framework for that to happen in a structured way.[15]

The act propelled a change in the way that the senior judiciary and Parliament interacted. The result was a change in the relationship to one of dialogue.

Democratic dialogue

Before the supreme court came into being, there was not an obvious need for a formal means of dialogue between the judiciary and the legislature. With the final institutional separation of the two, there were moves to craft a more structured means of contact to ensure each continued to understand the other and, indeed, hear from the other. There was a dual motivation. One was negative, inasmuch as dialogue was important to avoid misunderstandings between the two. The other was positive in terms of shared interests, especially in relation to the executive.

The means of contact was important in ensuring especially that the concerns of the judiciary could be conveyed to Parliament and that parliamentarians were alert to issues and gained input on policy deliberations that affected courts and the delivery of justice. This contact came to be facilitated through committees in both Houses. The House of Lords constitution committee has proved especially important. As Le Sueur and Simson Caird noted, it has come to serve as a forum for dialogue between parliamentarians and the judiciary and as a safety valve in times of tension between ministers and judges.[16] According to their analysis, the work of the committee achieves four main goals. One is as a facilitator, enabling senior judges to raise concerns. The lord chief justice, as well as the president of the supreme court (each often accompanied by their deputies), make annual appearances before the committee. The other roles are to hold ministers to account for their judiciary-related responsibilities, to call the senior judiciary to account, as on the handling of news media, and providing oversight of the new constitutional structure.[17]

A similar dialogue takes place with MPs through the justice committee in the Commons. Both committees hear not only from the head of the judiciary on a regular basis, but also take evidence from judges in the course of inquiries related to the courts and the administration of justice. The constitution committee undertook an inquiry into judicial appointments, later doing a follow-up inquiry, which resulted in a range of judges and lawyers appearing before the committee. The appearance of judges before parliamentary committees increased notably after 2003, the year in which the decision to create a supreme court was announced. As the research of Gee *et al.* has shown, in the ten years from January 2003, there were 148 occasions when oral evidence was given by seventy-two salaried judges. If the category is extended to include international and retired judges, as well as deputy high court judges and magistrates, the number rises to 185 who gave evidence.[18]

The two institutions have a shared interest in the protection of rights. Cases may be brought before the courts on grounds of an infringement of rights covered by the ECHR. Under the Human Rights Act 1998, the senior courts can issue declarations of incompatibility. They are dependent on Parliament enacting legislation to ensure law is compatible with their judgments. However, they can only issue judgments when cases are brought. Parliament is engaged when a measure affecting human rights is first introduced. Ministers have to certify that the bills they introduce are compatible with the ECHR. This again is where Parliament has developed a significant role through the use of a committee.

The Joint Committee on Human Rights (JCHR) is the principal means by which Parliament scrutinises bills to determine their impact on human rights and whether they do comply with convention rights. It also fulfils a wider, more proactive, remit in examining the scope and effectiveness of human rights protection in the UK.[19] There is thus a comity of interests between Parliament and the courts in keeping in check any encroachment on human rights by the executive.[20] Together, they have served to engender a culture shift in discussing and appreciating human rights. The joint committee has undertaken a range of inquiries into different aspects of rights, including subjects such as human trafficking, deaths in custody and counter-terrorism policy in respect of pre-charge detention. Especially salient in terms of the democratic dialogue, the committee has published guidance to government departments on how to respond to court judgments on human rights.[21] This entails not only responding within four months to a declaration of incompatibility, but also writing to the committee setting out its response, including the timetable for remedying any incompatibility. The committee has also made clear that it seeks the active involvement of civil society in its scrutiny of government responses. Through its work it has, in the words of its first chair, helped build in government a 'culture of justification' rather than one of assertion.[22]

The committee has also appeared to be instrumental in building a rights-based culture, reflected in a notable increase in references to human rights in both Houses, especially the Lords.[23] Equally importantly, the courts have taken note of the committee's work, not only on occasion noting them, but also utilising them as persuasive in reaching a decision. Hunt *et al.* identified fourteen instances where a majority of the court agreed with the reasoning of the JCHR.[24]

There has thus been a more structured relationship between Parliament and the courts, with notable contact through committees and a greater sensitivity to rights issues. Both Houses have been more alert to issues of human rights and have proved willing to challenge government, not least in terms of anti-terrorism legislation and pre-charge detention. The first defeat in the House of Commons of the Labour government under Tony Blair was on the government's attempts to provide for ninety-day pre-charge detention. The impact of Parliament in this context was summarised by Peter Riddell when discussing anti-terrorism legislation, observing that the government was likely to encounter problems with the House of Lords and the senior judiciary.[25] Parliament was in effect serving as a partner with the courts in the protection of rights.[26] The government had not only to anticipate the reaction of the courts, but also Parliament, when contemplating legislation that may impinge on the rights of citizens.

The relationship rests for its effectiveness upon each branch continuing to recognise the role of the other, in effect an element of mutual deference. There may be some tension at times deriving from legal doctrines, such as parliamentary privilege.[27] Court judgments in *Miller* (2016) and *Cherry/Miller (2)* (2019) engendered public and vehement criticism from some MPs who saw them as undermining Parliament's position, although former justice Jonathan Sumption noted that both served to uphold the position of Parliament against the executive.[28] In the *Cherry/Miller (2)* case, the supreme court was careful to distinguish challenging executive actions from parliamentary sovereignty. It was an unprecedented case – a 'one off' as the court president, Lady Hale, noted – but one to uphold constitutional orthodoxy.

Competing authority

The relationship of Parliament to the courts has contrasted with that of government, where the relationship has been more mixed. As we have seen, the courts have become more active in recent decades in reviewing the actions of ministers. Applications for judicial review grew in the 1990s and were notably high in the period from 2010 to 2013, peaking at over 15,000, though falling back since.[29] Although most applications for judicial review of ministerial decisions fail, there have been some high-profile cases of ministers having their actions struck down by the courts. In 1993, the House of Lords held a former home secretary, acting in an official capacity, in contempt of court for failing to comply with a court order in an asylum case. The case was significant because it meant that ministers could no longer rely on crown immunity to ignore a court order. Successive home secretaries found themselves falling foul of the courts. Jack Straw lost cases when he was home secretary and later when he was foreign secretary. In 2012, the high court found Home Secretary Theresa May in contempt of court for failing to abide by an undertaking to release a foreign criminal. The following month, she had to take emergency action after the supreme court ruled unlawful the UK border agency's points-based system for migrants.

Ministers did not always react with a good grace. In 2001, home secretary David Blunkett attacked interference by judges in political matters and raised the possibility of suspending the Human Rights Act. Prime Minister Tony Blair raised the possibility of amending the act and Jack Straw, as justice secretary, spoke of wanting to 'rebalance' the legislation.[30] Criticism of judges by ministers became such that, at one point, the lord chief justice, Lord Phillips of Worth Matravers, intervened to stress that the judges were doing their job in applying the law. The lord chancellor, Lord Falconer of Thoroton, reminded ministers not to interfere in judicial cases.[31] He nonetheless went on to stress the need for the executive and judiciary to recognise their respective roles. The courts, he said, must be sensitive to the needs of the state and the values of society. 'If the public lose confidence in where the balance is struck, then the system is undermined.'[32]

Following the *Miller* case in 2016, Lord Chancellor Liz Truss encountered significant criticism, not least from jurists, for failing to defend judges following media attacks on the members of the high court for its decision in the case. As lord chancellor, she was under a statutory duty to have regard to the need to defend the independence of the judiciary. In 2019, when there were fears ministers may ignore the European Union Withdrawal (No. 2) Act, Lord Chancellor Robert Buckland reminded ministers, including the prime minister, of their duty to uphold the rule of law.

There was a more extensive clash in September 2019 in the *Cherry/Miller (2)* case. Lord Justice McCloskey in Northern Ireland held that the prime minister's advice to prorogue Parliament was non-justiciable, as did the high court in England. Lord Doherty in the court of session in Edinburgh reached a similar judgment, but when this was appealed to the court of session, it held that it was justiciable and that the prime minister had acted improperly to 'stymie' Parliament and that his advice to the queen was therefore unlawful. The supreme court sided with the court of session. It distinguished parliamentary sovereignty from Parliament holding government to account and held that the length of prorogation prevented Parliament from fulfilling its constitutional duty. Prorogation, it held, was not a proceeding in Parliament, but something imposed on Parliament from outside.[33] The key point here for our purposes is that the court was not reviewing legislation, but the lawfulness of executive action. The judgment was crafted in such a way as to uphold the position of Parliament against the power of the executive. 'For this reason', wrote Sionaidh Douglas-Scott, 'despite alarm from some quarters, the judgment cannot be said to represent a deviation from the central tenets of the constitution. To the contrary, it upholds them. While a remarkable ruling, it is in this and other respects an orthodox one'.[34]

The prime minister said he would 'respect' the judgment, but nonetheless made clear that he disagreed with it. According to the BBC, 'A No 10 source said the Supreme Court had "made a serious mistake in extending its reach to these political matters" and had "made it clear that its reasons [were] connected to the Parliamentary disputes over, and timetable for" Brexit'.[35] The view that the court was straying into territory that was the preserve of ministers shaped the stance of the Conservative Party in the subsequent general election. The Conservative Party manifesto included a commitment to establish, in the first year of the new parliament, a constitution, democracy and human rights commission to examine the relationship between the government, Parliament and the courts. More pointedly, it included commitments to 'update' the Human Rights Act and to reform judicial review to ensure that 'it is not abused to conduct politics by another means or to create needless delays'.[36]

Conclusion

Though ministers work with the senior judiciary on the administration of justice, not least in the provision of court services, there are tensions arising from the greater judicial activism and constitutional reforms of recent decades. The creation of the supreme court has put the highest court at some distance physically from Parliament, while generating in response a more structured form of dialogue. This comity has enabled Parliament to act as something of a buffer in protecting the courts from executive attack and in developing a rights-based culture, developments most marked in the House of Lords, facilitated by former law lords, and lord chief justices, resuming membership of the House. This protective role has also been facilitated to some degree by behavioural changes, especially in the House of Commons, where MPs have become more independent in their voting behaviour. The government as a result is not able to take Parliament, especially the House of Lords, for granted in seeking to restrict or ignore court judgments. The respective autonomy of the branches has thus changed over time, with democratic dialogue now characterising the relationship between the legislature and the courts, but with competing authority marking at times, and notably since 2016, the relationship between the executive and the courts. One, so far, has helped limit the other. How far that continues, given the Conservative victory in the 2019 general election and the party's commitment in effect to limit the powers of the courts, remains to be seen.

Notes

1   Norton 2013b; Norton 2015a: 53.
2   See Norton 2006: 15–17.
3   Straw 2012: 538.
4   Dickson 2019: 78.
5   See Norton 2017c, 2019b.
6   White 2009: 36.
7   Norton 2005: 322.
8   Department for Constitutional Affairs 2003: 4.
9   Norton 1982: 134.
10 Norton 1982: 136–42.
11 Thomas of Cwmgiedd 2014: 2.
12 Thomas of Cwmgiedd 2017: 181.
13 Norton 2017c: 177–9.
14 [2004] 1 AC 816: 54.
15 Thomas of Cwmgiedd 2017: para. 17.
16 Le Sueur and Simson Caird 2013: 282.
17 Le Sueur and Simson Caird 2013: 304–7.
18 Gee *et al.* 2015: 113.
19 Norton 2013a: 154.
20 See Young 2009: 128.
21 Norton 2013a: 156.
22 Norton 2013a: 159.
23 Hunt *et al.* 2012: 19–26.
24 Hunt *et al.* 2012: 52.
25 *The Times*, 16 September 2005.
26 Norton 2013a: 164.
27 See Young 2017: 201–8.
28 BBC *Newsnight*, 16 January 2020.
29 Norton 2018a: 522.
30 Norton 2018a: 528.
31 Norton 2007: 15.
32 Falconer 2006.
33 [2019] UKSC 41: 24.
34 Douglas-Scott 2019; see also Elliott 2019.
35 *BBC News Online*, 24 September 2019.
36 Conservative Party 2019: 48.

Chapter 7

The law of Parliament: who polices the rules?

The courts interpret and apply acts of Parliament, that is, outputs of Parliament. What happens up to the point of enactment is primarily deemed a matter for Parliament. The courts recognise that Parliament, and each House, enjoys exclusive cognisance, that is, the capacity to resolve its own affairs, free from judicial interference. This capacity pre-dates the Bill of Rights 1689 and is not conferred by statute, but derives from the fact that Parliament, as the high court of Parliament, was considered to have its own distinctive law. Though lawyers have since moved away from accepting that there is a separate form of law, there is a case that, as Howarth has noted, 'Parliament, especially the Commons, operates its own legal system', though not one influenced by the legal system operated by the courts.[1] Further protection is provided by the Bill of Rights. Article 9 states that 'freedom of speech and debates or proceedings in Parliament ought not to be impeached or questioned in any court or place out of parliament'. This provision is seen as a core element of the constitution, providing protection for Parliament in undertaking its core task of debating and resolving issues without external interference.

On the face of it, this combination of common law and statutory protection makes Parliament master of its own domain. However, the position is not as clear-cut as this statement may suggest.

Neither exclusive cognisance nor proceedings in Parliament has been subject to a clear definition. The scope of exclusive cognisance and the meaning of proceedings in Parliament, given that it is protected by statute, are matters for the courts. The courts accept that those matters that fall within exclusive cognisance are solely for Parliament to determine and that they cannot question proceedings in Parliament. However, they have on occasion had to wrestle with, and determine, the contours of both concepts.

For Parliament, there is the challenge of using its powers of exclusive cognisance. It cannot change the protection accorded its proceedings guaranteed by Article 9, other than by statute, but it could alter or waive its powers falling within its exclusive cognisance. It has the more persistent task of organising its own procedures and determining how to police the rules it sets and to enforce its will. Within Parliament, a complex set of rules has developed to govern proceedings. Policing those rules in the House of Commons falls essentially to the chair and officials acting under the authority of the chair, but the rules may be challenged or changed by the House. The privileges of each House extend to the capacity to compel those outside Parliament to attend and provide evidence to enable it to carry out its tasks. The enforceability of the power to require witnesses to attend is now in question. Each House has penal powers, but the last time the Commons employed the power to impose a fine was in 1666 and to detain an individual 1880. Although the House has not repudiated those powers, it resolved in 1978 that it would use them sparingly. In 2018, the committee of privileges decided that, in considering whether a particular failure to appear before a committee constituted a contempt, if it found the case proved 'the maximum penalty it will recommend the House to impose is admonishment'.[2] Compelling someone against their will to appear before a committee may be open to challenge as incompatible with article 6 of the ECHR. Even if witnesses appear, can the House take action if they refuse to answer questions?

Proceedings in Parliament

The scope of the powers of each House to determine and enforce its privileges has come before the courts on a limited number of occasions. Although cases have been rare, the courts have not shied away from exercising their power to determine the meaning and limits of exclusive cognisance and proceedings in Parliament. However, neither they nor Parliament have provided a precise definition of either concept.

It is, though, possible to identify some common ground as to what is, and what is not, encompassed by the terms. As Lord Phillips of Worth Matravers, president of the Supreme Court, noted in the *Chaytor* case in 2010, although the jurisprudence was sparse,

> it supports the proposition ... that the principal matter to which article 9 is directed is freedom of speech and debate in the Houses of Parliament and in parliamentary committees. This is where the core or essential business of Parliament takes place. In considering whether actions outside the Houses and committees fall within parliamentary proceedings because of their connection to them, it is necessary to consider the nature of that connection and whether, if such actions do not enjoy privilege, this is likely to impact adversely on the core or essential business of Parliament.[3]

Anything falling within the formal recorded proceedings of the House – the agenda and what members say in debate or other scheduled proceedings – enjoys absolute privilege. (That protection extends now to those giving evidence to committees of the House.) The protection is not for the benefit of individual members, but for the House to fulfil its functions. Behaviour falling outside such proceedings, even if within either House, is not necessarily protected. If an MP speaks in a debate, the speech falls within the ambit of article 9. The MP cannot be sued for defamation or face any criminal or civil action. If the MP then walks across the chamber and physically assaults another MP or an official, the action is not protected by article 9. It does not constitute a proceeding in Parliament. In 2010, three MPs who had been charged with false accounting for submitting expenses claim forms to the fees office of the House of Commons for costs they had not incurred appealed to the UK supreme court. They did so on the grounds that their actions were protected by privilege, citing both article 9 and the exclusive cognisance of Parliament. The court held that the submission of claim forms did not fall within the protection of article 9, having no impact on the essential business of Parliament. Scrutiny of such claims by the courts 'will not inhibit any of the varied activities in which Members of Parliament indulge that bear in one way or another on their parliamentary duties. The only thing that it will inhibit is the making of dishonest claims'.[4]

In terms of exclusive cognisance, it was acknowledged that the dividing line between what was and what was not privileged was not easy to define. The judgment cited the report of the 1999 joint committee on parliamentary privilege that, to fall within the privileged category, the area 'must be so closely and directly connected with proceedings in Parliament that intervention by the courts would be inconsistent with Parliament's sovereignty as a legislative and deliberative assembly'.[5] The judgment went on to note that Parliament had by legislation and administrative changes largely relinquished any claim to have exclusive cognisance of administrative business. The processing of claims for expenses were administrative and the House made no claim that it fell within its exclusive cognisance. Furthermore, as Lord Rodger pointed out in a concurring opinion, 'for centuries the House of Commons has not claimed the privilege of exclusive cognisance of conduct which constitutes an "ordinary crime" – even when committed by a Member of Parliament within the precincts of the House'.[6] The House made no attempt in this case to do so. All the parliamentary authorities cited in the judgment supported the view that expenses claims had no close nexus with proceedings in Parliament. The appeal was rejected.

The issue also arose in 2019 in the *Cherry/Miller(2)* case in determining whether the ceremony of proroguing Parliament was a proceeding in Parliament. The president, Baroness Hale, said that, although prorogation was declared in the House of Lords, by lords appointed to form a royal commission, the lords were carrying out the queen's bidding. 'They have no freedom of speech. This is not the core or essential business of Parliament. Quite the contrary. It brings that core or essential business of Parliament to an end.'[7] It could not therefore be sensibly described as a proceeding on Parliament.

What these cases indicated was consensus as to what was clearly covered by privilege (determining the business, speaking in debates and other formally scheduled proceedings) and certain behaviour that was not protected from being brought before the courts (claiming expenses, part of an administrative procedure, and prorogation). What it did not resolve was the dividing line between behaviour that was privileged and that which was not. An instance of dispute as to what is or is not covered is an MP's correspondence. In 1957, an MP, George Strauss, wrote, on behalf of a constituent, to a minister criticising the London electricity board. The board threatened a libel action after the minister sought its comments and Strauss raised its action as a possible breach of privilege. The privileges committee decided that the MP's letter constituted a proceeding in Parliament and therefore privileged. However, the House, by a small majority, did not agree. In 1967, a select committee on parliamentary privilege concluded that the privileges committee had misdirected itself and that the issue should not have been the status of the letter, but whether there had been an obstruction likely to affect the parliamentary duty of the MP affected.

The Strauss case illustrates the problems of determining the dividing line, though in this case the discussion as to the status of the letter took place within Parliament. There is the potential for disagreement between Parliament and the courts as to where the line is to be drawn. One such case did arise in 1990. In *Rost* v. *Edwards*, the courts held that the Register of Members' Interests should not be considered a proceeding in Parliament. Concern over the judgment was expressed by a joint committee on parliamentary privilege in 2013 and endorsed by the government in its response to the committee's report. However, the government was not persuaded of the need for legislative clarification, given the infrequency of cases coming before the courts.

A case for change?

One of the most significant cases where the courts have had to determine Parliament's power to exercise its privileges was that of *Stockdale* v. *Hansard* in 1839, where the judges stood their ground in determining what fell within the scope of privilege. As the 1967 committee on parliamentary privilege recorded, there was a history of fruitless, and often undignified, conflicts between the courts and Parliament. The practice today is more one of not seeking to encroach on the domain of the other. However, the potential for conflict remains. Parliamentary committees have considered whether legislation is desirable. The 1999 joint committee recommended that parliamentary privilege be codified in statute, thus transferring considerable power to the courts. Another joint committee on parliamentary privilege in 2013 recommended against codification and 'embraced the virtues of evolution and adaptation'.[8] As Samson characterised it in evidence to the privileges committee of the Commons, the 1999 committee recommended legislation, whereas the 2013 committee recommended assertion.[9] The 2013 committee favoured some legislative changes, such as the replacement of the Parliamentary Papers Act 1840, but primarily argued for the House to act by resolutions and new standing orders to affirm the ability of select committees to secure the co-operation of witnesses and the power of the two Houses to investigate and, where necessary, punish contempts.[10] In the event, no action has been taken.

In practice, the courts are reluctant to encroach into what happens within Parliament. The courts may now, under a rule advanced in *Pepper* v. *Hart* in 1993, examine the parliamentary record to determine, in cases of ambiguity, the meaning of a particular provision. The court of appeal in 2002 in the case of *Wilson* v. *First Country Trust* went wider and looked at proceedings on a bill not as an aid to interpretation, but in order to find why Parliament had enacted a particular section. It was rebuked, and in robust terms, by the House of Lords. 'It is for Parliament alone to decide what reasons, if any, need to be given for the legislation that it enacts', declared Lord Hope of Craighead. 'The quality or sufficiency of reasons given by the promoter of the legislation is a matter for Parliament to determine, not the court.'[11] Conversely, both Houses adopt the rule of not commenting once a case is before the courts. There was no disagreement between the courts and parliamentary authorities as to the status of claims for expenses in the *Chayter* case. The relationship in this context is thus one of friends, rather than strangers or foes (Chapter 6). However, the potential for conflict remains, not least given changing understandings of what is encompassed by the exclusive cognisance of Parliament.

Enforcing the rules

The relationship between Parliament and government, and how each House of Parliament operates, is largely governed by conventions, practices and precedent, rather than by statute law. The constitutional lawyer and MP, Sir Kenneth Pickthorn, once observed that 'procedure is all the poor Briton has, now that any Government which commands 51 per cent of the House of Commons can at any moment do anything they like with retrospective or prospective intentions'.[12] Procedure, though, is extensive. Parliament is highly institutionalised. The procedures, rules and precedents have accumulated over time and are drawn together in *Erskine May*, a guide first published in 1844 and variously updated since.[13] The 25th edition was published in 2019.[14] It runs to more than 1,000 pages.

The rules of procedure both favour and limit ministers. Ministers enjoy certain privileges by virtue of being ministers and government enjoys hegemony in determining the parliamentary timetable. Only ministers can move certain motions, such as Ways & Means resolutions. The current precedence accorded government in proceedings derives from rule changes of the late nineteenth century and the reforms introduced by Arthur Balfour as leader of the House in 1902.[15] As Josef Redlich observed in 1908, the past quarter-century had witnessed the strengthening of the powers of the Speaker, 'the continuous extension of the rights of the Government over the direction of all parliamentary action in the House', and the suppression of the role of the private member.[16]

Although ministers enjoy privileges, they are also constrained by both processes and procedures. The process by which law is approved – the different stages in each House, the fact that bills must normally be considered consecutively and not concurrently by the two Houses, the gaps normally between each stage – constrains government. Bills cannot be passed quickly, other than in exceptional circumstances and usually with the agreement of the principal parties. Opposition parties normally like to scrutinise bills, focusing on partisan points of contention. The House of Lords usually considers the detailed provisions in some depth. Government business managers have to factor in how long it will take for a bill to get through all its stages. Most bills have to pass within the course of a session (usually one year), otherwise they fall, so ministers have to limit the number of bills introduced at the beginning of each session. In institutional terms, Parliament is a notable constraint on government.[17]

Ministers and backbenchers act within established procedures, but without themselves being experts on those procedures, nor arbiters as to their use and interpretation. Parliamentary rules are policed by clerks and, in the House of Commons, the Speaker.

How they interpret and apply the rules can affect outcomes and the role of the Speaker can be critical in constraining or enhancing the role of the House in relation to the executive. Some Speakers have sought to enhance the position of members, be it in relation to an obstructive minority (Speaker Brand) or to government (Speaker Bercow). Rulings by John Bercow in 2019 brought the Speaker's powers to interpret the rules and standing orders of the House to the fore. The situation in the self-regulating House of Lords is different in that there is no authority to challenge other than the House itself. The House not only sets the rules, but also is the body responsible for determining what they mean.

In the Commons, the application of the standing orders and rules by the Speaker have rarely proved controversial. They are largely premised on two principal bodies, the government and the opposition, facing one another, with the government enabled to get its business considered and the opposition entitled to be heard. There is, as we have noted (Chapter 1), an equilibrium of legitimacy, each recognising the position of the other.[18] The balance favours government in getting its business. Given that the government normally enjoys a majority in the House, there is no conflict between the executive and the House.

The situation, however, becomes less clear where there is a minority government and a majority in the House seeking to achieve an outcome opposed by the government. This was notably the case in 2019 over the issue of Brexit, with an ad hoc majority of different opposition parties, independents and dissident government backbenchers seeking to determine the business of the House and to wrest control of policy from government. The Speaker was drawn into political controversy and accused of bias in favour of those opposed to Brexit, interpreting what constituted a neutral motion and the term 'forthwith' in a manner seen to favour their cause. His rulings enabled amendments to be moved to motions hitherto deemed unamendable. In whatever way he interpreted the rules, he was likely to be criticised, given that he could not please both a minority government and a majority in the House. In the event, his interpretations, some in line with precedent and some not, were challenged on the grounds they favoured those opposed to a 'no deal' Brexit. Without his rulings, the majority would not have been able to gain control of the timetable and enact two European Union (Withdrawal) Acts opposed by the government.

Enforcing its will

Each House has powers to enforce its will in relation to its own members and to those outside the House. The House of Commons has the power to expel and to suspend members. The House of Lords in 2009 determined that the power to suspend members until the end of a parliament, although not employed since the seventeenth century, remained (and utilised it). Under the 2015 House of Lords (Expulsion and Suspension) Act, it acquired greater powers to suspend and, for the first time, the power to expel a member. One of the key cases in which the courts were engaged in determining the scope of exclusive cognisance was *Bradlaugh* v. *Gosset* in 1884. The House of Commons detained Charles Bradlaugh, a newly elected MP who was an atheist, and resolved that he not be allowed to take the oath, even though the Parliamentary Oaths Act 1866 required an MP to do so. The high court took the view that, as it was to do with the internal procedures of the House, interpretation of the statute was a matter for the House.[19]

Both Houses have established disciplinary procedures and committees to consider whether members should be subject to suspension or expulsion, with motions for such action being based on reports from the committees. Each House has now a commissioner for standards to investigate and report on allegations that a member has breached the House's code of conduct. Members who are suspended from the Commons are not paid for the period of suspension. Peers who are suspended cannot claim an attendance allowance (peers are not salaried and can claim only an attendance allowance and travel expenses) given that they are barred from attending for the period of suspension.

The only notable problem for each House investigating and imposing sanctions on a member is if the member ceases to be a member, be it by electoral defeat or resignation in the Commons, or by resignation in the Lords. Until 2014, peers could not resign or retire from membership, but under the House of Lords Reform Act 2014 they can now do so. (By 2020, more than 100 peers had made use of the provision.) Arguably, the inability to act against an MP or peer who has transgressed the rules, but has left the House, is not that significant, given that the most severe sanction that could normally be employed is expulsion. In 2019, the privileges committee of the Commons recommended that one member, Keith Vaz, be suspended for six months – the longest suspension ever recommended – but the 2019 general election intervened and Vaz did not stand for re-election. In 2019, the House of Lords agreed, after showing some reluctance to do so, to suspend a peer, Lord Lester of Herne Hill. Lord Lester then retired from the House. Where there is a lacuna is in respect of any member who retires having failed to repay money inappropriately claimed, an issue following the expenses scandal of 2009.

Each House can act against members who are deemed to breach the rules of the House. Each can also act to protect members from pressures from those outside the House. The freedom of each House to debate freely, unfettered by external influences, has proved problematic in terms of defining when members have been subject to undue external pressures. It has also proved problematic in terms of action for any breach of its privilege by individuals outside the House.

As Geoffrey Marshall noted, MPs in modern political history are influenced by external forces in the form of political parties. Members vote with their parties and may be subject to threats from the party whips or the party organisation. Over time, there have been claims that whips have resorted to physical threats and even propelling reluctant MPs into the desired division lobby. Members may not like it, but they do not regard pressure from the whips as constituting an infringement of privilege. However, others seeking to influence how MPs speak and vote have on occasion been subject to claims that their activity is a breach of privilege. The impact of party 'injects an air of unreality into every occasion on which the writer of a postcard or the editor of a newspaper is told that he is guilty of impeding or intimidating Members of Parliament in the exercise of their freedom of vote and utterance. The victim may well ask himself what he has done that can stand comparison with the exertion of the Whips' office'.[20] Marshall noted a tendency of members in the mid-twentieth century to be possibly over-sensitive to criticism. 'To judge solely by the number of occasions on which issues of privilege have been raised in the House', he wrote, 'there would seem to have been an increase over the last twenty years in the tendency of the world outside Westminster to trespass on the Commons' power and dignity (the Lords seem not to have been much upset)'.[21] Claims of breaches of privilege by individual members have rarely been upheld.

It has become less common for individual members to raise pressures from outside Parliament as constituting breaches of privilege, though during the EU referendum of 2016 there was a notable increase of breaches of criminal law, with threats of, or actual, violence to MPs. One MP, Jo Cox, was murdered. Others were subject to online abuse and harassment and some physical threats or intimidation.

The issue of privilege has been more salient in recent decades in ensuring that committees of the House are able to fulfil the duties conferred on them. Committees have the power to summon 'persons, papers and records' and a warrant can be issued for anyone refusing a command to give evidence to a committee of the House. Each House, as we have noted, has formal powers to punish those who commit contempt by failing to comply. But, especially in the light of human rights legislation, to what extent is the writ to attend enforceable? A combination of public pressure and the implied threat of action of failing to respond to a Speaker's warrant, delivered by a member of the staff of the Serjeant at Arms, has usually proved sufficient for those summoned to comply. When in 1992 the two sons of the late Robert Maxwell, who had been found to purloin the pension fund of his company, were summoned to appear before the House of Commons social security committee, they turned up, but they declined to answer any questions. Their lawyer, George Carman QC, said they were exercising their right of silence. Others have attended, after some indication they may decline, not least in recent years business figures such as Rupert Murdoch (chair of News Corporation), Mike Ashley (chief executive of Sports Direct Group) and Sir Philip Green (former owner of retailer BHS). Attendance, as in the case of the Maxwell brothers, has not always resulted in witnesses providing substantive answers, but they have attended.

What could the House do if they had failed to appear? Dominic Cummings, director of the Vote Leave campaign in the 2016 EU referendum campaign, declined to appear before the Digital, Culture, Media and Sport Committee in 2018, with the committee seeking action by the House to require him to appear. He was reported to the House and, following a report from the Committee of Privileges (2019), a motion was agreed holding him in contempt and admonishing him, but no formal sanctions were imposed.

There have been calls for the powers of the House to be strengthened, not least through statute. The privileges committee in its 1967 report argued for the power of the House to commit someone to prison and to impose a fine to be affirmed. As we have noted, the 1999 joint committee recommended that the powers be codified in legislation. The 2013 committee, favouring flexibility, did not. Nothing happened with either report.

The two joint committees identified two ways forward. One is to legislate, following the examples of Australia and New Zealand, although neither of these has legislated for a full codification. Each has passed an act confirming the legislature's penal jurisdiction rather than transferring it to the courts.[22] The other way is to follow the preference of the 2013 joint committee and opt for assertion, introducing procedures that would make requiring witnesses to attend where summoned (as distinct from being invited) to do so largely immune to judicial intervention. By essentially following the requirements of article 6 of the ECHR to ensure a fair hearing, with a right of appeal and to have a legal representative present, it is unlikely that the courts would entertain a challenge. Pursuing such a path would not necessarily constitute a significant departure given that committees in any event are keen to ensure fairness. 'Fairness is applied daily in committees.'[23]

Calls for the powers to summon witnesses to be made statutory are objected to on the grounds that it would make proceedings justiciable, thus bringing the courts into matters falling within the exclusive cognisance of Parliament. However, as we have noted, article 9 of the Bill of Rights is a statutory provision, amenable therefore to judicial interpretation, and the courts, though recognising exclusive cognisance, determine its scope. There is therefore the potential, occasionally realised, for some conflict between Parliament and the courts. However, each is keen to avoid encroaching on the domain of the other. Each House is wary of taking action that would provoke judicial intervention. The courts recognise that, while they are there to interpret the law, it is ultimately Parliament that makes law.

Notes

1   Howarth 2017: 312.
2   Committee of Privileges, House of Commons 2019: 4.
3   [2010] UKSC 52: para. 47.
4   [2010] UKSC 52: para. 48.
5   Joint Committee on Parliamentary Privilege 1999: para. 247.
6   [2010] UKSC 52: para. 122.

Governing Britain

7   [2019] UKSC 41: para. 68.
8   Sampson 2017: 301.
9   Committee of Privileges, oral evidence, 22 October 2019.
10   Joint Committee on Parliamentary Privilege 1999: paras 280–1.
11   [2004] 1 AC 816 [117]; see Norton 2017c: 177–9.
12   *HC Deb.* 8 February 1960, col. 70.
13   See Evans 2017.
14   Natzler 2019.
15   See Redlich 1908: 193–212.
16   Redlich 1908: 206.
17   Norton 2001: 21–5; Norton 2013c: 6–7.
18   See Norton 2001: 27–8.
19   See Howarth 2017: 315.
20   Marshall 1967: 44–5.
21   Marshall 1967: 44.
22   See Sampson 2017: 302–3.
23   Eve Sampson, memorandum to the Privileges Committee, 2019, SCC0019.

Chapter 8

Fixed-term Parliaments: fixed or not so fixed?

When Parliament came into being in the thirteenth century, it was a body that met infrequently and sometimes there were long periods when it was not summoned. Although in the fifteenth century, Henry IV and Henry V generally held annual parliaments, meetings thereafter became rarer. 'Henry VII held only seven parliaments in a reign of twenty-four years and could claim it as a virtue that he held so few.'¹ Charles I (1625–49) ruled without a Parliament for eleven years before his need for money became too great. When a Parliament was summoned, formally it remained in existence, unless dissolved, until the demise of the monarch. Parliament did seek to legislate to control meetings and the length of parliaments. Triennial Acts were enacted in 1641, 1644 and 1694. The last of these, the Meeting of Parliament Act, stipulated that Parliament was to meet each year, with an election after three years. This proved to be rather too short and encouraged continuous electioneering, so in 1716 an act was passed – the Septennial Act (known, because at the time bills were dated by year of introduction rather than passage, as the Septennial Act 1715), limiting the life of a Parliament to seven years. This was reduced to five years by section 7 of the Parliament Act 1911. Within that period, the prime minister could seek a dissolution and new election. (Up to 1918, the decision was ultimately that of the cabinet and since that time of the prime minister.)[2] In the period from 1945 to 2010, the average length of a Parliament was three years and ten months.[3]

Mostly, the prime minister's choice was unfettered, generally selecting a time deemed propitious for government. A premier with a clear working majority would typically seek an election after four years, or five years if the opinion polls were not favourable. However, if a government was returned with a small or a non-existent majority, forming a minority administration, the life of a Parliament could be short, as with the Parliament returned in 1950: Prime Minister Clement Attlee sought another election the following year. Harold Wilson as prime minister presided over two short Parliaments: that of 1964, which lasted until 1966, and that of February 1974 which did not even see the year out, with a second election that October. The 1966 general election gave Wilson a large working majority, whereas that of October 1974 did not.

The prime minister's discretion was, though, fettered if the government lost the confidence of the House. By convention, a government that lost the confidence of the House either resigned or opted for a general election (see Chapter 3). Requesting an election was the practice in the twentieth century on the rare occasions that it happened. The only time an explicit motion of no confidence was put and carried was in 1979, precipitating a general election.

The discretion accorded prime ministers in determining the date of a general election attracted criticism. It was viewed as giving the incumbent an unfair advantage. The prime minister could not only select a date when the government was ahead in opinion polls, but also announce the election at a time that disadvantaged the opposition in planning an election campaign. The governing party could plan, knowing when the request for a dissolution would be made, whereas opposition parties could be left guessing. 'Governments', declared Deputy Prime Minister Nick Clegg in 2010, 'have been distorted, paralysed, hobbled and handicapped over and over again by the capricious manner in which Prime Ministers have played cat and mouse with the British people and with the legislature about when elections should be held ... This is debilitating to good government; it destroys good government'.[4]

There were also practical problems deriving from calling an election well before a parliamentary session ended, resulting in what was known as the 'wash-up', with bills not yet passed either being rushed through, with agreement between the parties, or dropped. Whereas selecting the date of an election could disadvantage the opposition electorally, it did at least have some leverage in the wash-up in determining legislative outcomes.

The prime minister's power to decide when the next general election would occur led to calls for fixed-term parliaments, the length of each Parliament being set. This would both remove the prime minister's capacity to manipulate an election to favour the government as well as remove the problems associated with the wash-up. There would be greater certainty for legislative, strategic and financial planning, given the fourth and fifth sessions of a parliament would run their full length.[5]

The case for fixed-term parliaments became more vocal towards the end of the twentieth century.[6] Labour MPs Austin Mitchell (in 1983), Tony Banks (in 1987 and 1992) and Jeff Rooker (1994) pursued private members' bills on the subject. Both the Labour and Liberal Democrat manifestos in 1992 included proposals for fixed-term parliaments.

Parties in government were less inclined to support the proposal. The governing Conservative Party in the 1990s was not minded to lose its capacity to decide when an election occurred. Prime Minister Margaret Thatcher gave short shrift to questions asking if the government would legislate on the subject.[7] When the Labour Party was returned to office in 1997, it failed, despite its previous stand, to act on the issue. Some MPs kept pressing for change. Labour MP Tony Wright introduced a private member's bill in 2001, as did Liberal Democrat David Howarth, supported by senior Liberal Democrat MPs such as Nick Clegg, in 2007. They failed to make any headway.

What changed the situation was the failure of the 2010 general election to produce a single-party majority. One outcome of the negotiations between the Conservative and Liberal Democrats was a concession by the former. It agreed to the introduction of a bill to provide for fixed-term parliaments. The coalition agreement declared:

> We will establish five-year fixed-term Parliaments. We will put a binding motion before the House of Commons stating that the next general election will be held on the first Thursday of May 2015. Following this motion, we will legislate to make provision for fixed-term Parliaments of five years. This legislation will also provide for dissolution if 55% or more of the House votes in favour.[8]

The measure was designed to demonstrate that the coalition would last a full Parliament. It helped convey a sense of stability. The motivation for a super-majority to trigger a general election was to reassure the Liberal Democrats that the Conservatives would not suddenly and unilaterally seek an early election to their disadvantage.

In the event, there was no binding motion introduced, principally because the government realised there was no one to be bound by such a motion: prerogative powers cannot be constrained by declaratory motions of the House of Commons. It proceeded instead to introduce a bill to provide for parliaments of five-year terms, though with provision for an early election if two-thirds of all MPs (rather than 55 per cent) voted for it. The 55 per cent figure had looked anomalous by international standards, whereas a two-thirds threshold was used in the devolved legislatures. The coalition agreement made no mention of an early election if the government lost the confidence of the House. The bill sought to remedy this by embodying the existing convention, providing for an early election if 'on a specified day the House passed a motion of no confidence in Her Majesty's Government (as then constituted)' and if within fourteen days the House had not passed 'any motion expressing any confidence in any Government of Her Majesty'. It provided that the Speaker was to certify if a motion was one of no confidence and that a period of fourteen days had elapsed without a motion of confidence being passed.

The bill included no definition of what constituted a motion of no confidence. The government took the view that the Speaker would recognise and certify whether a motion was one of confidence and could inform MPs before the vote. However, this gave rise to two problems.[9] One was that it may bring the Speaker into realms of political controversy if it was disputed as to whether a motion was one of confidence. The other was that it could bring the courts into adjudicating in the event of a dispute over the Speaker's certificate. As the political and constitutional reform committee in the House of Commons reported, there may be a problem if a motion of confidence in the government was defeated and the Speaker certified it as a vote of no confidence. The House would have demonstrated that it did not have confidence in the government, but it would not have 'passed' a motion as required by the terms of the bill.[10]

Given these problems, the bill was amended during its passage in the House of Lords to provide greater clarity. As a result, the Fixed-Term Parliaments Act 2011 stipulates that an election will take place on the first Thursday in May every five years, but provides, in section 2, that there may be an early general election if either:

(1) two-thirds of all MPs (if the motion is divided on) vote for the motion 'That there shall be an early parliamentary general election'; or
(2) the motion 'That this House has no confidence in Her Majesty's Government' is passed and if, within fourteen days, the motion 'That this House has confidence in Her Majesty's Government' is not passed.

The first provision thus introduces a super-majority, whereas the second requires a simple majority to pass. The super-majority is a high one in that, if not passed unanimously without a vote, it requires two-thirds of all MPs, and not simply two-thirds of those voting, for it to be carried. The effect is to make the opposition, and backbenchers, veto players in that they could vote against to prevent the two-thirds hurdle being achieved.[11] Abstention would have the same effect, though some members would have to vote against in order to ensure a division.

If there is an early general election, the election clock is reset, rather than the new Parliament serving for what remains of a five-year term. If an early election takes place before May, the next election takes place in May in four, rather than, five years. If after May, it is five years from that May. If the early election takes place in May, the new Parliament lasts for five years. If in any other month, it lasts for between four and five years.

The effect of the provisions mean that the act provides not so much for fixed-term parliaments as semi-fixed-term parliaments.[12] It has also generated problems of interpretation. It shows the problems of seeking to translate a convention into statute. The act can be analysed in terms of its effect, problems and calls for change.

Effects

The effects of the act did not work out as intended. With fixed terms, there would only have been one general election between the act coming into force (in September 2011) and 2020. In the event, there were three (2015, 2017, 2019). The Parliament in which the act was passed lasted the stipulated five years, which was the principal intention of the coalition partners. However, in April 2017 Prime Minister Theresa May sought and obtained a two-thirds majority (MPs voting by 522 votes to 13) for an early election. Rather than, as intended, strengthening her majority, the election left the Conservatives in a minority, reliant on the support of a third party, the Democratic Unionist Party.

The ease with which the prime minister achieved an early election on a date of her choosing confirmed in the eyes of some observers that the act was not going to mark much change from what preceded it. During debate on the prime minister's motion, Conservative MP Sir Edward Leigh declared, 'It would be a brave man or woman who voted against this motion. The Fixed-term Parliaments Act 2011 is therefore seen to be an emperor without clothes—it serves no purpose, and many of us have questioned it for many years'.[13]

In the event, the emperor turned out to have clothes. Two years later, in September 2019, Theresa May's successor, Boris Johnson, faced with a House of Commons in which he could not prevent supporters of Brexit taking control of the timetable and enacting legislation designed to prevent a no-deal Brexit (see Chapter 4), sought an early election on three occasions. When the motion was first put, on 4 September, 298 MPs voted for it and 56 voted against. It thus fell short of the two-thirds majority of all MPs (434) required to trigger an election. The prime minister tabled the same motion for the following Monday (9 September), with opposition parties stating they would not vote for it because it may prevent Parliament sitting and being able to prevent the UK leaving the EU on 31 October with no deal agreed. The result of the division was 293 votes to 45, again well short of the two-thirds threshold. The third occasion was on 28 October, when the result was 299 votes to 70, again short of the required majority. Opposition MPs thus effectively exercised a veto, denying the prime minister the general election on the date he sought. According to former prime minister Tony Blair, Labour leader Jeremy Corbyn had 'the most sensitive part of Johnson's political anatomy in his hands'.[14]

During the debate on the second motion, one Conservative MP declared that the effect of the act 'is now to trammel this Government and our Prime Minister in a very Kafkaesque trap: he is finding it very difficult to govern but is unable to call a general election. I very much hope that the first act of the new Parliament will be to abolish the Fixed-term Parliaments Act'.[15]

In the event, the government decided to introduce a short bill to provide for an early general election on a stipulated date (12 December 2019), which would require only a simple majority to pass. The government lacked an overall majority (the whip having been withdrawn from twenty-one Conservative MPs the previous moth) and so was dependent on the support of one or more opposition parties. Given that Scottish National Party (SNP) MPs wanted an election and would vote with the government, there appeared to be a majority for the bill. The opposition decided not to oppose it and on 29 October it was given an unopposed second reading and taken for its remaining stages on the same day. An amendment, to provide for the election on 9 December, was defeated by 315 votes to 295. After clearing the House of Lords, the bill received royal assent and Parliament was dissolved at the start of 6 November.

The Fixed-Term Parliaments Act has thus led to a novel situation. Before 2011, the monarch could decline a prime minister's request for dissolution, though at no point in modern British politics was that power exercised. The act transferred the crown's power to the House of Commons. The prime minister could seek a general election, but it was now dependent on MPs to vote for it. They have proved willing to exercise the power to deny a prime minister's request.

The alternative for a prime minister who wants an early election is either to engineer a vote of no confidence in one's own government or to pass a bill setting a date for a general election, the provisions of the Fixed-Term Parliaments Act notwithstanding. Each requires only a simple majority to pass. The problem with the first is political in that it would require government MPs voting no confidence in their government. The problem with the second is that the bill would need to go through all the bill stages in each House, which takes time if the measure is opposed and the House declines to pass a business motion to facilitate prompt passage. In the event, in October 2019, the government opted for this second course successfully.

Problems

The act, as was demonstrated by the events of 2019, has various ambiguities or difficulties that were not thought through or anticipated. The bill was, according to the Political and Constitutional Reform Committee in the House of Commons, ill thought through and rushed.[16] The policy behind it, noted the House of Lords Constitution Committee, 'shows little sign of being developed with constitutional principles in mind'.[17] There was, it recorded, an important distinction between the immediate concern of the coalition government that it should continue for five years and the long-term issue of fixed-term parliaments. The first of these could be achieved under existing constitutional arrangements, whereas the second constituted a significant constitutional change.

The provision stipulating that, in the event of a vote of no confidence, an early general election takes place if, within fourteen days, a confidence motion has not been passed, created both an ambiguity and a problem.

The ambiguity that emerged was as to who could form a government and seek a vote of confidence in the wake of a vote of no confidence being carried. The act is silent as to whether it can be the existing government, revamped (with some ministerial changes) or not, or an alternative government. The opposition is the alternative government, so the leader of the opposition may feel entitled to be called to Buckingham Palace and invited to form a government.

The problem deriving from the provision was that it stipulated fourteen days without any qualification. It made no provision for weekends or bank holidays. The clock begins ticking once the no confidence motion is carried. If the motion is carried towards the end of December, there are practical problems in recalling Parliament at Christmas to pass a motion of confidence. The government could, if it wished, just sit the fourteen-day period out, and not request a recall of Parliament. There is no requirement under the act for the motion to be put, only that it requires to be put and carried if an early election is to be avoided.

If the government, having had a no confidence motion carried, did decide to resign, then an alternative government would have to be formed quickly in order to gain a motion of confidence. The new prime minister would have to be in place by day 14 because there has to be a government in which confidence can be expressed. In the autumn of 2019, as we have seen (Chapter 3), some MPs, drawn from different parts of the House, discussed the possibility of uniting behind a figure, other than the leader of the opposition, who could command a majority, and conveying this to the palace. In the event, none of this came to fruition, but the fact of its discussion – and its potential consequences – highlighted the potential constitutional dilemmas that could result from the ambiguous provisions of the act.

There is also a problem deriving from section 2(7) which provides that, if there was an early election, the polling day is to be one appointed by the queen on the recommendation of the prime minister. This proved contentious in 2019, when Boris Johnson sought an early general election. One of the reasons the opposition withheld its support was in case the prime minister delayed polling until after the stipulated deadline (of 31 October) for the UK's exit from the European Union. Once the deadline had been extended, it proved willing not to oppose an election on 12 December.

What also proved to be politically contentious, though the potential was not realised at the time, was the power of the prime minister to advise that Parliament be prorogued, which was retained in the act. Section 6(1) states: 'This Act does not affect Her Majesty's power to prorogue Parliament'. As we have noted (Chapter 3), the power proved contentious in 2019 when Boris Johnson decided to advise the queen to prorogue Parliament for five weeks, which, had the advice not been declared unlawful, would have limited the time available to Parliament to discuss Brexit.

Calls for change

The effects and perceived problems of the act led to various calls for it to be amended or repealed. During its passage in the House of Lords, concerns about its merits led some peers to press for a sunset clause, that is, providing for it to cease to have effect after a certain date, unless renewed by Parliament. To avoid a possible defeat on the issue, the government agreed to the inclusion of a provision for the act to be reviewed in 2020. Under section 7, the prime minister has to appoint a committee for this purpose, with a majority of the members having to be MPs. If appropriate, the committee is to make recommendations for the repeal or amendment of the act and the prime minister must make arrangements for the publication of the committee's findings and report.

In 2019, in anticipation of the review, the House of Lords Constitution Committee began in inquiry into the workings of the legislation. In evidence to the committee (by this writer), it was pointed out that there were four options, the four Rs – retain, repeal, rejig or replace.

Retention would be to keep the act as it stands. Although widely criticised, retaining the act constitutes the default option if none of the alternatives is agreed. Repeal is advocated by some parliamentarians without realising that simply repealing it creates a serious lacuna. In 2014, Labour peer Lord Grocott introduced a private member's bill – the Fixed-Term Parliaments Act 2011 (Repeal) Bill – with one substantive clause: 'The Fixed-term Parliaments Act 2011 is hereby repealed.' The following year, Conservative MP Sir Alan Duncan, supported by some senior Conservative and Labour members, introduced an identical bill in the Commons. The problem is that, if the act is repealed, the prerogative power may resume (the view among constitutional authorities is that it would), but the legislation limiting the life-time of a Parliament – the Septennial Act, as amended by the Parliament Act – does not. The result is that Parliament would continue indefinitely, until such time as the prime minister advised the monarch to dissolve it.

To avoid such an eventuality requires either amending the existing act – that is, rejigging it – or replacing it with a new act. Amending the existing act could entail, for example, changing the provisions for an early election, such as reducing the two-thirds vote of all MPs to two-thirds of those voting. It could stipu-late who could form the government for the purpose of seeking a confidence vote following a vote of no confidence. Given the nature of the criticism of the existing measure, this may not be sufficient to meet the demands of those parliamentarians seeking change.

A new act could in effect recreate what existed prior to 2011 – that is, having a maximum length of five years, with the prime minister able to recommend a dissolution within that period – but that would need to be specified in its provisions. The problem with such a measure is that it would be open to the criticisms levelled before 2011. It would strengthen, or would be assumed to strengthen, the power of the prime minister. Addressing these concerns may necessitate some limitation on the prime minister's discretion being worked into the bill. The maximum length of a Parliament may also be revisited. Whether the lifetime should be capped at four rather than five years was a live issue during the passage of the bill in 2011. Finding a con-sensus in both Houses on a new bill may thus prove problematic. Both main parties in the 2019 general election committed to the repeal of the act. Neither party thus supports its continuation, but reaching agreement on what should exist in its place may prove more challenging.

Notes

1 Mackenzie 1968: 31.
2 Markesinis 1972: 72–84.
3 Constitution Committee, House of Lords 2010b: 16.
4 Constitution Committee, House of Lords 2010b: 11.
5 See Political and Constitutional Reform Committee, House of Commons 2010: 4, and 2013: 4–8.
6 See Norton 2000: 122–3.
7 Norton 2000: 123.
8 HM Government 2010: 26.
9 Norton 2016b: 11–12.
10 Political and Constitutional Reform Committee, House of Commons 2010: 14.
11 Norton 2016b: 3–18.
12 Norton 2014: 203–20.
13 *HC Deb.* 19 April 2017, col. 681.
14 Blair 2019: 14.
15 *HC Deb.* 9 September 2019, col. 626.
16 Political and Constitutional Reform Committee, House of Commons 2010: 5.
17 Constitution Committee, House of Lords 2010b: 8.

Chapter 9

Choosing, and removing, a prime minister: who decides?

The choice of the prime minister rests formally with the sovereign – the holder is the principal adviser to the monarch – but the means by which the holder has been chosen has changed over time. Initially, the choice was in the personal gift of the sovereign. He or she could hire and fire as they wished. With the advent of a mass franchise and the growth of organised political parties in the nineteenth century, it became the practice to select the leader of the majority party in the House of Commons. The constitutional position remained unchanged in that the sovereign looked to someone who could command a majority in Parliament to grant supply and assent to the measures brought forward by the ministers on behalf of the crown.

For most of the twentieth century, the party leader who stood ready to be called upon to form a government was either chosen as leader by the party's MPs, as was the case with the Labour Party, or 'emerged' in the case of the Conservative Party until 1965, when the party switched to election by the parliamentary party. In the 1980s, the Labour Party moved to election of the leader by the party membership. The Conservatives followed suit after their election defeat in 1997 and employed election by party members for the first time in 2001.

Once a prime minister is in place, they remain in office until they resign or are dismissed. They may resign at a time of their choosing or the departure may be involuntary. Formally, they can be dismissed by the monarch, but since the gradual withdrawal of the monarchy from active engagement in government, that no longer occurs in practice, though it remains as an ultimate option. In practice, the prime minister may be dismissed by the electors, with the return of another party to office, or may be forced out by their own party.

Choosing a prime minister

The first prime minister is generally recognised as being Sir Robert Walpole, though he disliked the title. He was the first of fifty-five people to hold the post (fifty-three men and two women) up to and including Boris Johnson. He was also the longest serving, holding office for twenty-one years from 1721 to 1742. He appears to have been favoured by both George I and George II because of his parliamentary skills. 'Conversely, the fact that he was the King's minister and retained the confidence of the King was crucial to his support in parliament.'[1] The monarch continued to run government. Walpole, for instance, did not choose ministers and there was no concept of collective responsibility. Over time, the position developed in importance, but the holder needed to retain the confidence of the monarch as well as of Parliament. The premier was very much the choice of the monarch, though the capacity to get the king's business in Parliament was a prime influence in the appointment.

In the nineteenth century, the monarch usually sought advice before inviting someone to be prime minister.[2] This was often necessary because it was not always clear who was the obvious candidate to form a government. The Conservatives in opposition, for example, had not one leader, but a leader in each House. By the twentieth century, the parties each had a leader, so in most cases there was no problem for the monarch in knowing who to call in the event of the prime minister resigning or losing an election. The monarch chose as premier whoever could command a majority in the House of Commons. That person was and is usually obvious – the leader of the majority party.

Constitutional dilemmas

The relationship, however, is not problem-free in that there may be circumstances in which it is not clear who can hold the confidence of the House of Commons. There are three principal circumstances where this may happen. One is where a party has no recognised leader to succeed a resigning incumbent, as in earlier times, or the outcome of an election is unclear or during a Parliament a government implodes or loses its majority. In these cases, there is an incumbent who stays in office until a successor is appointed. The second is where there is an immediate vacancy as a result of the prime minister dying or choosing to resign immediately without waiting for a new leader to be elected. The third is where the leader chosen by the party may not enjoy the confidence of the parliamentary party.

No clear leader. The first circumstance mentioned – uncertainty as to who should succeed a resigning premier – was an issue at different points in the twentieth century in respect of the Conservative Party. When the leader resigned, the new leader 'emerged'. It was usually clear who was effectively number two in the party and ready to take over. If in office, that person was summoned to Buckingham Palace and once appointed was endorsed as leader by a party meeting. However, in four out of ten leadership successions between 1902 and 1963, there was no one person that had clearly 'emerged' at the time of the vacancy.[3] In 1911, the two leading contenders gave way to a compromise candidate (Bonar Law). In 1922 there were two contenders to succeed the dying Bonar Law – Lord Curzon and Stanley Baldwin – with the king sending for Baldwin. As we noted in Chapter 3, the resignation in 1957 of Sir Anthony Eden and in 1963 of Harold Macmillan, both on health grounds, left the queen in some difficulty as no clear leader had emerged on either occasion. After taking advice, she summoned Harold Macmillan in 1957 and, more controversially, the Earl of Home in 1963. The controversy generated on both occasions, and the embarrassment to the crown through having to exercise a choice, led to Sir Alec Douglas-Home (as Lord Home had become) instigating a review of the rules for choosing a leader. In 1965, it was agreed to move to electing the leader whenever a vacancy occurred. The rules were first employed that year. In 1975, the rules were further changed, providing for the leader to be subject to re-election, initially annually and later changed to if challenged.

As a result, the first circumstance is no longer likely to pertain. A prime minister remains in office until the party elects a new leader. Once elected, the outgoing premier goes to Buckingham Palace to resign and the successor summoned to be appointed.

However, the prospect of uncertainty remains in the event of an indecisive general election outcome or the government losing its majority during the lifetime of a Parliament. There was uncertainty as to who would be able to lead government following the outcomes of the general elections in February 1974 and 2010. In both cases, it was left to inter-party discussions to resolve, to avoid bringing the monarch into having to make a choice. In 1974, when the Conservatives lost their overall majority, Edward Heath explored forming a pact or coalition with the Liberal parliamentary party. When Liberal MPs declined to participate, he resigned and the queen sent for the leader of the opposition, Harold Wilson. In 2010, there were discussions between Labour and the Liberal Democrats, and between the Conservatives and the Liberal Democrats. Once it was clear that the Conservatives and Liberal Democrats had negotiated a coalition agreement, the prime minister, Gordon Brown, headed to Buckingham Palace to tender his resignation.

The danger of the sovereign being drawn into political controversy is perhaps most marked when premiers have lost their majorities during Parliaments. In 1916, Prime Minister Asquith came under pressure from his chancellor, David Lloyd George, and Conservative ministers in the wartime coalition. Asquith resigned and the king, George V, invited the Conservative leader, Bonar Law, to form a government. There was then a conference of leading ministers at Buckingham Palace, which failed to reach agreement. After the meeting, Bonar Law ascertained that leading Liberals would not serve under him and he declined the king's commission. Lloyd George was summoned and formed a coalition government.

In 1931, the Labour cabinet of Ramsay MacDonald fell apart over the issue of retrenchment. MacDonald had alerted the king to the fact that he may have to resign. George V consulted the Conservative and Liberal leaders. Sir Herbert Samuel, the Liberal leader, suggested a national government if a Labour cabinet could not deliver the economies needed.[4] When the cabinet split, MacDonald tendered its resignation and after a conference of all three leaders at Buckingham Palace, a national government was announced. As Harold Nicolson recorded, 'It was suggested in some quarters that the King, in urging the leaders of all three Parties to unite in forming a National Government, had gone beyond his constitutional powers'.[5] Nicolson argued that the king was acting on advice: the recommendation that MacDonald continue in office and form a national government originated with Samuel and had been supported by Baldwin. It was clear, though, that the king was an active broker in the discussions that took place and had urged to parties to come together.[6]

A similar danger arose in 2019 after the government of Boris Johnson lost its parliamentary majority after the whip was withdrawn from twenty-one MPs and there was the prospect of a vote of no confidence in the government being carried. Given a lacuna in the Fixed-Term Parliaments Act, it was not clear what would happen if prime minister resigned. Would the queen be expected to invite the leader of the opposition to form a government and see if the new government could gain a vote of confidence within the fourteen-day period following the first vote? There was speculation that there may be an attempt to pass a motion expressing no confidence in the government, but not in the form of words stipulated by the act. If passed, it would engage the convention that the government resign, the option of asking for an election having been removed by the act. In such circumstances, it would normally be expected that the leader of the opposition would be invited to form a government. However, there were discussions between different parties and independent MPs as whether to put forward a senior backbench MP as someone who could command a majority in the House. If such a coalition did come into being, who would convey the name of the preferred candidate to the queen and what would the prime minister do if he was not willing to abide by the convention and resign? What would happen if a motion of no confidence in the form stipulated in the act was passed, but the prime minister refused to resign and sought to sit out the fourteen-day period, even if there was an alternative who could command majority support? There was no precedent to draw on and, as we have noted (Chapter 3), the position of the queen was a sensitive one after the prime minister's request for a lengthy prorogation had been struck down by the supreme court.

No leader. There are also problems if there is a sudden vacancy in the office. The formal position (selection by the crown) and constitutional norms (there has to be a prime minister) have not necessarily kept up with the political reality (election by party members). What happens if a prime minister dies or resigns and refuses to stay in office until a successor is elected, given that election of a leader by party members may take weeks or months?

The last prime minister to die in office was Palmerston in 1865, at a time when the choice of prime minister could still be determined by the sovereign and when there was no perceived urgency to appoint a successor. Days could elapse between a prime minister resigning and a new one being appointed. In the twentieth century, two prime ministers resigned shortly before dying – Campbell-Bannerman (who, having resigned, died in No. 10) and Bonar Law – but at a time when the choice of successor could be made quickly, not being dependent on a lengthy process of election, be it by MPs or by party members.

The election of party leaders, be it by MPs or a wider electorate – especially the latter – created a problem that was not provided for, though it was foreseen in the 1970s by the queen's private secretary. What happens if a prime minister dies in office? It was a question that exercised various cabinet secretaries.[7] In 1984, while the Conservative Party conference was taking place in Brighton, cabinet secretary Sir Robert Armstrong heard the news that there had been a bomb explosion at the Grand Hotel, housing the prime minister and members of the cabinet. He spent half an hour not knowing whether the prime minister was alive or dead and, if dead, what to do. His successor, Sir Robin Butler, also wrestled with a similar problem when the cabinet was in session and No. 10 was hit by an IRA mortar attack. Despite their concerns, no protocols were put in place to deal with the situation in the event of the prime minister being killed or succumbing to a fatal heart attack.

In the event, what to do in the event of the incumbent dying or being incapacitated had been considered by Sir Martin Charteris, the queen's private secretary, who recognised the implications following the Conservative Party changing its rules for the election of a leader in 1975. The election process could take some time. Should there be an interim prime minister and, if so, how would they be chosen? He held a meeting with officers of the Conservative 1922 Committee to discuss the situation and a memorandum was agreed,[8] although in subsequent decades few, if any, in positions of authority appeared to know of its existence.

The memorandum had two principal features.[9] One is that it was premised on having an interim, or acting, prime minister.

The Duke of Wellington did briefly serve as such in 1834 while Sir Robert Peel returned from Rome, but that is the only occasion. There is no obvious constitutional bar to the monarch inviting someone to serve in such a capacity. The other is that the person so chosen should not be a candidate for the leadership. (Serving would provide the candidate with an unfair advantage, or possibly an unfair disadvantage if having to campaign while holding the reins of government.) At the time, a possible neutral figure was agreed to be the lord chancellor (a senior figure in the Lords, who could not be a potential candidate). With the Constitutional Reform Act 2005 enabling the lord chancellor to be an MP, and hence a potential leadership figure, that no longer applies.

Given that, if a sudden vacancy arises, the presumption is that the cabinet would proffer the name of someone who was not a candidate for the party leadership and who would be acceptable as interim prime minister. That person could then serve for the period that it takes for the party to elect a new leader. The process could be short-circuited, avoiding the need for an interim premier, if only one person was nominated as party leader and could therefore be promptly invited to form a government. Either outcome would avoid the monarch being drawn in to having to make a choice.

Party members versus the parliamentary party. There is another effect of election of the party leader by members of the party not always being compatible with the constitutional requirements for being prime minister. A prime minister rests on the confidence of House, which derives usually from having a party majority. The rules for electing the party leader by the party membership in both the Conservative and Labour parties[10] mean that it is possible for a leader to be elected who does not enjoy the support of most members of the parliamentary party. The Conservative rules, however, do allow for the leader to be removed by the party's MPs. The Labour rules do not.

Under the Conservative Party rules, if there are more than two candidates nominated, MPs hold eliminating ballots until there are only two candidates and those two names are then put to the party members. In 2001, the first time the rules were utilised, the winning candidate, Iain Duncan Smith, never enjoyed clear support in the parliamentary party – he had effectively emerged in a three-way split, narrowly edging out leading MP Michael Portillo in the final ballot among MPs and then winning against Kenneth Clarke in the ballot of party members. Two years later, MPs triggered a confidence vote, made possible under the 1998 rules, which Duncan Smith lost. In the 2016 leadership contest, Andrea Leadsom withdrew from the contest, ostensibly because of comments she made about the other candidate, Theresa May, being childless, but it was believed she was influenced by the realisation that she lacked the support of the majority of Conservative MPs. Theresa May was the first Conservative prime minister to be subject to a confidence vote. She won, in December 2018, by 200 votes to 117.

These rules do, though, as we have noted, mean that a leader that does not enjoy the support of the parliamentary party can be removed and, if in office, therefore resign as prime minister. This continues the position that pertained from 1975 when the leader could be voted out by the party's MPs. There is a more serious problem in terms of the Labour Party rules, in that a leader cannot be removed by a vote of no confidence by the party's MPs, but only by a vote of the party membership. Labour leader Jeremy Corbyn, elected by party members in 2015, never enjoyed the support of most Labour MPs. In 2016, they passed a vote of no confidence in his leadership by 172 votes to 40, but it had no effect and he continued as leader. He was subject to a leadership challenge the same year, but the party membership re-elected him by 313,209 votes to 193,229 for his challenger, Owen Smith.

This creates a problem in that if the Labour Party won a general election, with most of those elected as Labour MPs not having confidence in the leader, the person invited to form the government would not enjoy the confidence of the House of Commons. This, though, would not by itself be a bar to becoming prime minister as confidence is taken to exist unless the House votes no confidence in the government. However, it could engender difficulty if Labour MPs made clear their continuing lack of confidence in the leader.

More importantly, such a lack of support could have constitutional implications in exceptional circumstances, such as those existing in 2019. If the House of Commons was to express no confidence in the government, either in the form stipulated in the Fixed-Term Parliaments Act or otherwise, and the leader of the opposition lacked the confidence of his own party, should the queen invite the latter to form a government? The expectation would normally be that the opposition leader would be summoned, not least because of the absence of an alternative. However, as we have seen, there were discussions as to an alternative candidate for the premiership. The challenge in those circumstances would be to reach agreement, including with the leader of the opposition, as to a candidate, in order to avoid the monarch having to make what would be a politically contentious choice.

Removing the prime minister

On occasion, the issue may not be how to fill a vacancy, but how to get rid of the incumbent. What are the means, if any, by which a prime minister who wishes to remain in office may be removed, other than through a general election? The prime minister serves not only formally at the pleasure of the sovereign, but in practice at the pleasure of the electors and, in between elections, at the pleasure of their party. Leaders are put in place by the party and may be removed by the party.

The prime minister may cease to be party leader, and hence prime minister, as a result of informal pressure from within the party or from being ousted under party rules. In practice, the removal of the party leader while prime minister has been confined principally to the Conservative Party. Liberal Prime Minister Herbert Asquith was forced out in 1916 in favour of his chancellor David Lloyd George. Since then, it has been only Conservative prime ministers that have suffered a similar fate; perhaps not surprisingly given that the party has been in office for more time than any other party. The Labour Party expelled Ramsay MacDonald as party leader after he agreed to head a national government in 1931, but he continued as prime minister. The party has lost two leaders through death (Hugh Gaitskell and John Smith), both while in opposition, but none, MacDonald apart, has been forced out, either in opposition or government.

Before the Conservative Party changed the rules on electing the leader in 1975, under which a leader could be voted out, the only way a leader could be removed was by pressure from within the party. The popular perception was that a leader was ousted by a visit from the 'men in grey suits', in essence, a delegation from the executive of the 1922 Committee or other party grandees. The only flaw with this perception was that it never happened.[11] Only after the 1975 rules change were leaders removed by the party's MPs.

In 1931 and 1947, there were messages transmitted via intermediaries that it was time for the leader (Baldwin in 1931, Churchill in 1947) to retire, but they came to nothing. Both carried on for some years until handing over to their chosen successors. Other leaders resigned because they were ill or worn down by the strains of office and internal party conflict (Balfour, Bonar Law, Eden, Macmillan, Douglas-Home). The Suez crisis effectively destroyed Eden's premiership, but it also affected his health and he gave up office following medical advice. Austen Chamberlain – the only Conservative leader in the twentieth century prior to 1997 never to be prime minister – gave up after the collapse of the Lloyd George coalition in 1922. Neville Chamberlain gave up the premiership, but not the party leadership, after a parliamentary vote that reflected a major loss of confidence in his government by Conservative MPs. (He gave up the leadership some months later when terminally ill.) Balfour and Douglas-Home were the subject of backbench criticism – there was a BMG (Balfour Must Go) movement – but went at the time of their choosing. The announcement by Douglas-Home in 1965 that he was giving up the leadership took the parliamentary party by surprise.

Since 1975, three leaders have been voted out (Edward Heath in 1975, Margaret Thatcher in 1990 and Iain Duncan Smith in 2003), but only one (Thatcher) was prime minister at the time. Margaret Thatcher had been under pressure because of her stance on European integration, which split the Conservative Party, and on the community charge (or 'poll tax') which was highly unpopular in the country. She was challenged for the leadership in 1989, being re-elected over a 'stalking horse', little known backbencher Sir Anthony Meyer, but subject to a serious challenge the following year from former defence secretary Michael Heseltine. Heseltine mounted a major campaign, with Thatcher failing to spend time rallying supporters in the House. After falling short of victory by four votes in the first ballot, she announced her resignation, becoming only the second Conservative leader to be voted out by the party's MPs and the first prime minister to suffer that fate.

Two of her successors faced re-election votes – John Major in 1995 and Theresa May in 2018 – with both leaders winning, though Major only just exceeding the threshold he had set himself and May resigning within months of the contest. The introduction of formal rules for leadership elections in the Conservative Party – rendering the leadership, as one MP put it in 1975, leasehold rather than freehold – has meant that leaders now appear more vulnerable to being ousted by their own MPs than was previously the case. Prior to the 1975 rule change, if the prime minister was determined to stay on in the face of sustained backbench criticism, they could seek to do so (though, as we have seen, they may eventually decide it was time to go), but now MPs can remove them decisively. Under the rules as now exist, if a leader loses a vote of confidence, they are out and denied the right to seek re-election.

Those who see the UK as having an 'elective dictatorship' tend to focus on the dictatorship and not the elected element. Prime ministers are reliant on the electorate and on their own MPs to stay in office. The support of the former is necessary, but it is not sufficient to remain in Downing Street. Julian Amery once observed that a good jockey rides a difficult horse. Some leaders have suffered the indignity of being unseated by their parliamentary parties. Others have stayed astride, but on a frisky and at times close to runaway horse.

Notes

1   Taylor 1998: 10.
2   Keith 1952: 27–37.
3   Norton 1996b: 145.
4   Nicolson 1952: 461.
5   Nicolson 1952: 466n.
6   Nicolson 1952: 465.
7   Norton 2016c: 23–5.
8   Norton 2016c: 30–2.
9   Norton 2016c: 30–2.
10 See Heppell 2008, 2010.
11 Norton 1996b: 147.

Chapter 10

A deputy to the prime minister: a deputy but not a successor?

The monarch appoints a first, or prime, minister. There is thus clearly a head of government. But what happens if the prime minister is away, temporarily indisposed, or tied up exclusively on business that means they are not able to deal with other matters of state? On the premise that someone needs to be running government, who, if anyone, stands in for the prime minister?

There may be benefits to having a second-in-command. On occasion, the media have described a senior politician as 'deputy prime minister'. However, the existence of the royal prerogative, with the selection of the prime minister remaining formally within the gift of the sovereign, has meant that no office holder is an automatic successor if the premiership becomes vacant. Someone may be chosen by the prime minister to deputise for them on occasion, but without any right of succession.

Before the Second World War, a senior member of the cabinet was on occasion invited to act as deputy prime minister while the premier was ill or abroad. When Prime Minister Andrew Bonar Law was taken ill in 1923, it was arranged that in his absence 'Lord Curzon should act as deputy Prime Minister'.[1] In 1927, foreign secretary, Sir Austen Chamberlain, was asked to fulfil the role by Prime Minister Stanley Baldwin while Baldwin was visiting Canada. Similarly, in 1929, when Ramsay MacDonald went to the United States and Canada, Chancellor of the Exchequer Philip

Snowden was designated to carry out the role. However, no one was styled as deputy prime minister while the prime minister was in the country and physically able to run the government.

Since the 1940s, prime ministers have on occasion appointed someone to act on a continuing basis as their second-in-command. Those chosen for the role have been given the title of deputy prime minister, appointed first secretary of state, or simply served *de facto* as deputy prime minister, but without being formally styled as such. At other times, the prime minister has done without selecting anyone to fulfil the role, selecting a cabinet colleague on an ad hoc basis to fill in for them, for example at prime minister's question time, when they are abroad.

Deputy prime minister

The first time a senior minister was given the title of deputy prime minister while the prime minister was conducting affairs of state in Downing Street was in 1942 when Labour leader Clement Attlee was so styled. He also held the posts, successively, of lord privy seal, dominions secretary and lord president of the council, positions that enabled him to receive a salary. He was referred to as deputy prime minister by the press and was recognised officially as such by *Hansard* for the purpose of answering parliamentary questions.[2] Such a designation, though, was seen as exceptional, the product of coalition and wartime exigencies. In the event of Conservative Prime Minister Winston Churchill dying in office, it was not expected that Attlee, leader of the Labour Party, would succeed him. Churchill had advised the king that in the event of his death, Foreign Secretary Anthony Eden should be his successor.

For decades thereafter, the sensitivities as to the sovereign's prerogative in choosing a prime minister meant that no one was formally titled as deputy prime minister, even though there was often a senior minister who was generally regarded, including by the prime minister, as deputy to the premier. The position of the person so designated was perhaps most concisely put by Macmillan in 1962, when he said: 'This is not an appointment submitted to the Sovereign but is a statement of the organisation of Government.'[3,4]

Those generally recognised as falling in this category – deputy prime ministers in all but formal name – were Herbert Morrison (1945–51), Anthony Eden (1951–5), R. A. Butler (1962–3), William Whitelaw (1979–88), Geoffrey Howe (1989–90) and David Lidington (2018–19) (Table 10.1).[5] Although variously so described in the press, the designation never appeared in the list of cabinet offices.

The informal status of 'deputy prime minister' remained ambiguous, rarely conferred, and was described by Marshall and Moodie as a 'dubiously respectable title'.[6] Sensitivity to the royal prerogative continued to affect the conferment of the title as late as the 1980s. Geoffrey Howe was offered it in 1989, but he was then contacted by the prime minister's private secretary, Charles Powell,

Table 10.1 Deputy prime ministers

Clement Attlee	1942–5
Herbert Morrison	*1945–51*
Sir Anthony Eden	*1951–5*
R. A. Butler	*1962–3*
William Whitelaw	*1979–88*
Sir Geoffrey Howe	*1989–90*
Michael Heseltine	1994–7
John Prescott	2001–7
Nick Clegg	2010–15
David Lidington	*2018–19*

Those names in italics recognised as serving as deputy prime minister, but not formally styled as such.

to be told that Buckingham Palace 'had had a little difficulty in accepting the official description "Deputy Prime Minister". They were proposing to follow the precedent of Eden with Churchill and use the form of words: "Sir Geoffrey will act as Deputy Prime Minister". Was that all right?'[7]

However, the situation changed in the 1990s and there was a move, in effect, from an informal to a formal designation, with Michael Heseltine in 1995 being officially styled as deputy prime minister and answering parliamentary questions in that capacity. The same applied to John Prescott from 2001 to 2007. The office of deputy prime minister was created in the cabinet office in July 2001, though from 2003 until 2006 the deputy prime minister resumed the responsibilities he had from 1997 to 2001 as secretary of state for the environment, transport and the regions. When Liberal Democrat leader Nick Clegg was titled deputy prime minister during the period of coalition government (2010–15), there was a regular slot in question time for questions to the deputy prime minister.

This brief history identifies ambiguities arising from the title. Despite an 'office' of the deputy prime minister having been created in 2001, there is no salaried ministerial post of deputy prime minister. Sensitivities to the royal prerogative still shape the status. It remains formally a title conferred on an individual. Those on whom the title is conferred still have to be appointed to a salaried ministerial post. Nick Clegg, for example, throughout the period of coalition government held the senior post of lord president of the council, which not only conferred a salary, but also a leading position in the precedence of office holders. (The prime minister can determine the pecking order of ministers in the cabinet, but posts such as lord president of the council, Archbishop of Canterbury, and Speaker of the House of Commons have leading places on state occasions.) Attlee, as we have noted, was lord privy seal and then lord president of the council.

First secretary of state

If the designation of someone as deputy prime minister appears a little confusing, the picture is further blurred by the fact that a senior minister may be appointed as first secretary of state.

In December 2017, Damian Green resigned from government as first secretary of state. The position was as little understood when he resigned as when he had first been appointed six months earlier. Only eleven people have held the post since it came into existence (Table 10.2) and it has often been confused with the title of deputy prime minister.

The position of first secretary of state came into being in 1962. As part of his extensive cabinet reshuffle, known as the 'Night of the Long Knives', Prime Minister Harold Macmillan moved R. A. Butler from his post as home secretary and let it be known that he was to act as deputy prime minister. However, given that there was no recognised post of deputy prime minister, Macmillan proposed that Butler take the position of 'secretary of state'. Butler penned a pained letter to Macmillan 'to put my anxieties about

Table 10.2 First secretaries of state

R. A. Butler	July 1962 – October 1963
George Brown	October 1964 – August 1966
Michael Stewart	August 1966 – April 1968
Barbara Castle	April 1968 – June 1970
Michael Heseltine	July 1995 – May 1997
John Prescott	June 1997 – June 2007
Peter Mandelson	June 2009 – May 2010
William Hague	May 2010 – May 2015
George Osborne	May 2015 – July 2016
Damian Green	June 2017 – December 2017
Dominic Raab	July 2019 –

the plan you propose for me'.[8] He noted that there would be no precedence deriving from the title. 'I will therefore lose my position as senior Secretary of State, as Home Secretary, and also all my connection with the Court and my duties with the Queen.' He wrote that he would have no departmental responsibilities, other than for continuing to deal with Central Africa. 'Furthermore, without a classical office such as Lord President, I shall be out on a raft … I know what this means: one has a personal assistant and inadequate staff to transact business. I, therefore, think I shall be out on an African limb, as there has never yet been any clearly defined position for an undefined deputy.'

The consequence was that in the new cabinet list he was designated as first secretary of state. Butler in his memoirs makes no mention of the exchange with Macmillan, but simply records:

> Nominally, indeed, my position was enhanced: I gave up the Home Office but was named First Secretary of State and invited to act as Deputy Prime Minister, a title which can constitutionally imply no right to the succession and should (I would advise, with the benefit of hindsight) be neither conferred nor accepted. Save only for the Central African Office … I had no executive department to control; my responsibilities were, so to speak, supernal – specific or general as the Prime Minister might from time to time determine.[9]

The press were more interested in him being asked to act as deputy prime minister and then and since there has been confusion as to Butler's position. Both D. R. Thorpe and Robin Harris,[10] for example, assert that Butler assumed the post of deputy prime minister ('in name and not just fact' according to Harris), but the only appointment was as first secretary of state. There has been continuing confusion similarly as to the position of first secretary. There is little or no reference to it in texts on ministers and limited reference in the memoirs of those appointing, or being appointed, to the post. In his study of the office of secretary of state (the constitutional fiction being maintained that there is only one), A. J.

C. Simcock deals with the first secretary of state in a few lines. He describes it as 'a sidelight', and erroneously claims that the post originated in 1964, when George Brown was appointed to the position.[11]

When Brown was appointed, he interpreted the position as denoting 'who was in fact deputy to the premier',[12] claiming that, although the title continued to be conferred, 'with my departure from the Government it ceased to signify the Deputy Prime Minister'.[13] There is no authoritative source to confirm this interpretation and the prime minister, Harold Wilson, made no comment on the point in his memoir of the 1964–70 government.[14]

The essential distinction between first secretary of state and deputy prime minister is that the former is a ministerial post. One is appointed to it. According to the *Cabinet Manual*: 'A minister may be appointed First Secretary of State to indicate seniority. The appointment may be held with another office. The responsibilities of the First Secretary of State will vary according to the circumstances.'[15] Whereas deputy prime minister is a title, the only part of first secretary of state that is titular is 'first'. As a secretary of state, the holder receives seals of office[16] and the salary of a secretary of state under the Ministerial Salaries Act. (Although the salary of the first holder of the office, R. A. Butler, had to be met through a supplementary estimate.)[17] As explained in the *Cabinet Manual*, the designation indicates precedence. Barbara Castle, when she returned to cabinet in 1974, recorded that she had been moved down the cabinet table: 'no longer the central position I had as First Secretary'.[18]

Is it anything more, then, than a way of denoting precedence in cabinet ranking? In some respects, it is easier to say what it does not entail than what it does. It entails no departmental responsibilities and has no implications in terms of House of Commons procedure. In respect of its place within government, it appears a somewhat paradoxical position: in effect, a minister without portfolio who is a secretary of state. This was raised in 1963, when the opposition initiated a short debate on the status of the first secretary when the supplementary estimate to cover the cost of the new post came before the Commons. The constitutional lawyer, Sir Kenneth Pickthorn (Conservative MP for Carlton), queried whether Butler was arguing that all secretaries of state are equal, the position being formally indivisible, or that the post denoted that the title distinguished one secretary of state from the others. He went on:

> We should also know how a Secretary of State, of all animals, can be without a portfolio. It is possible to have cows without horns and all sorts of other animals many of which I would not wish to mention, without what are generally assumed to be their characteristic marks, but how one can have a Secretary of State without a portfolio completely defeats me.[19]

Butler had observed that the duties of all secretaries of state were interchangeable, but then went on to contend that he deputised for the prime minister, not least in relation to matters related to Europe. He continued:

> There are many other duties which, in deputising for the Prime Minister, I perform in Government, and I should like to draw the hon. Gentleman's attention to the fact that in a Government of whatever complexion it is rather useful to have Ministers without Portfolio who can perform duties within that Government of correlation, co-ordination and chairmanship of committees.[20]

Butler thus expressed the constitutional conundrum identified by Pickthorn, but also touched upon the utility of the position for a prime minister. There are two perceived advantages to the occupant of 10 Downing Street of being able to make someone first secretary of state. The same applies to the designating someone as deputy prime minister, other than the fact that the title holder also needs to be appointed to a ministerial post in order to receive a salary. The advantages to the prime minister are functional and political.

Benefits to the prime minister

The first benefit is to enable a senior minister to serve the prime minister, but without having responsibilities as a departmental secretary of state. It thus leaves the holder free to perform one or more of the tasks adumbrated by Butler – 'correlation, co-ordination and chairmanship of committees'. Butler saw his own role especially in terms of co-ordination. 'My experience is that, together with my duties in Central Africa, I can do better coordination in the present Conservative Government, placed as I am as First Secretary of State, than I could in charge of a great Department of State.'[21] Holders have notably been used to chair cabinet committees. This was a good part of the role accorded Michael Heseltine in 1995, though also encompassing a co-ordinating role: 'Heseltine's job was to combine the chairing of several Cabinet committees with a central role alongside Major coordinating and "selling" government policy.'[22] John Prescott's role similarly combined co-ordination with chairing cabinet committees. As the prime minister, Tony Blair, explained in 2002:

> As First Secretary of State, the Deputy Prime Minister will continue to deputise for me as required, drawing on the resources of other parts of the Cabinet Office as necessary. He oversees the work of the Social Exclusion Unit, which reports to me through him. He is also responsible for the Regional Co-ordination Unit and the nine Government offices of the Regions. I have asked him to be responsible for a White Paper on Regional Governance …
>
> The Deputy Prime Minister chairs Cabinet Committees on domestic affairs and on the nations and regions; and Sub-Committees on social exclusion and regeneration and on energy policy. He also chairs the newly established Ministerial Group (MISC18) on WSSD and continues to chair the Committee on the Environment.[23]

The answer was given in order to define the duties of the deputy prime minister, thus compounding the confusion as to the two roles. The first part of the answer was essentially the same as that given by John Prescott in answer to a similar question when the office of the deputy prime minister was established.[24]

Chairing committees was the principal role of Damian Green. As Thornton and Kirkup put it, he was looked to for the purpose of minding the shop when prime minister Theresa May was unavailable. 'More significantly, he was a mostly off-stage manager of government, a ubiquitous figure on Cabinet committees, and a key fixer of the deal between the Conservatives and the DUP [Democratic Unionist Party]'.[25] The holder may also be asked to stand in for the prime minister at prime minister's question time. The first secretary of state also has status in dealing with other ministers, in that by protocol they have to come to him or her. William Hague, for example, found his status useful when the prime minister, David Cameron, asked him to organise anniversary events for VE Day. As first secretary of state, he was able to co-ordinate and bring ministers together.

It also leaves the holder free to carry out other tasks assigned by the prime minister, though if these are ministerial roles the relevant ministerial position is given. When someone queried why it was deemed in order to discuss Butler's responsibilities for dealing with Central Africa during discussion of the supplementary estimate, the deputy chairman held that 'It is now part of the responsibilities of the First Secretary'. Kenneth Pickthorn immediately interjected 'Not as First Secretary'.[26] Other than Green, all first secretaries have held some other ministerial responsibilities.

Second, its political use is to enable the prime minister to send a signal as to the status of the holder. Appointing a first secretary of state or conferring the title of deputy prime minister is a way of indicating seniority. Combining the post of first secretary of state with title of deputy prime minister conveys how significant the person is in the eyes of the prime minister – it is a demonstrable indication of trust. Although George Brown interpreted his appointment as first secretary as indicating that he was deputy prime minister, he was not invited to act as such and he is not included in the list of those deemed to be deputy prime minister. Appointing him as first secretary served to assuage Brown's sensitivity as to his position without upsetting senior figures who were not always well disposed towards Brown (or his ego). Peter Mandelson may also be seen to fall into a similar category, the prime minister, Gordon Brown, being willing to accord Mandelson senior billing in government, but without causing controversy within the ranks of the Labour Party by designating a demonstrably controversial figure also as deputy prime minister. Having the post of first secretary of state and the title of deputy prime minister at the prime minister's disposal thus adds to the premier's arsenal of patronage in government.

There has also been a political use in the distinctive circumstances of coalition. This was when being able to have a deputy prime minister and a first secretary of state may be seen to have its greatest political utility. Under the coalition government of 2010–15, it enabled the prime minister, David Cameron, to signal who was the most senior Conservative cabinet minister, the title of deputy prime minister having gone to Liberal Democrat leader, Nick Clegg. Foreign secretary (later leader of the House of Commons) William Hague was appointed first secretary, a position he held throughout the period of coalition. This is the only occasion on which there was a deputy prime minister separate from the first secretary of state.

In short, among secretaries of state, the first secretary is *primus inter pares*. The seniority derives from the formal position. With the deputy prime minister, the seniority may be seen as a combination of whichever ministerial post is conferred (such as lord president of the council) and the political clout derived from enjoying the prime minister's confidence, assuming such confidence exists and is perceived to exist. The invitation to Sir Geoffrey Howe in 1989 to be titled deputy prime minister caused confusion in respect of the prerogative, but more significantly was seen as compensation for being removed from his post as foreign secretary. He was not seen to enjoy the prime minister's confidence – the prime minister's press secretary, Bernard Ingham, made some disobliging comments, describing it as no more than 'a courtesy title'.[27] Howe resigned the following year.

Not a successor

It is important to emphasise the constitutional position of both the title of deputy prime minister and the post of first secretary of state. Neither confers a right to succeed the prime minister in Downing Street. As we have seen (Chapter 9), if the prime minister resigns, whether voluntarily or involuntarily, the succession is determined in practice now by the governing party's membership and previously by the party's MPs, though formally the decision of the monarch remains unfettered. By convention, she appoints whoever the party elects to succeed the outgoing leader. The convention keeps the monarch free of political controversy. Formally, the sovereign's hands are not tied and in practice neither are the hands of the party members in electing a new leader. Holding the title of deputy prime minister or the post of first secretary of state does not confer any clear advantage. History would suggest the opposite. No first secretary of state has so far gone on to become prime minister. Neither have most of those seen as, or formally styled, deputy prime minister. Being number two in government has mostly proved to be the pinnacle of a politician's career, not a stepping stone to being number one.

Notes

1   Nicolson 1952: 375.
2   As, for example, *HC Deb.* 9 September 1942, cols.168–9w; House of Commons Library 2013: 2.
3   *HC Deb.* 19 July 1962, col. 633.

4   Macmillan went on to say 'It follows a very high precedent, for it was exactly the arrangement made by my right hon. Friend the Member for Woodford (Sir W. Churchill) when Sir Anthony Eden was appointed Deputy Prime Minister'.

5   See Thornton and Kirkup 2017.

6   Marshall and Moodie 1967: 138.

7   Howe 1994: 590.

8   Reproduced in Howard 1987: 292.

9   Butler 1973: 234.

10 Thorpe 2010: 523; Harris 2011: 442.

11 Simcock 1992: 550.

12 Brown 1972: 90–1.

13 Brown 1972: 91.

14 Wilson 1971.

15 Cabinet Office 2011: para. 3.12, p. 22.

16 Each Secretary of State receives three seals (Simcock 1992: 535). When William Hague was appointed leader of the House of Commons in 2014, a position that did not qualify as a secretary of state, he had to receive seals as a secretary of state.

17 *HC Deb.* 19 March 1963, col. 328.

18 Castle 1980: 39.

19 *HC Deb.* 19 March 1963, col. 327.

20 *HC Deb.* 19 March 1963, col. 323.

21 *HC Deb.* 19 March 1963, col. 323.

22 Seldon 1997: 588.

23 *HC Deb.* 1 February 2002, col. 567w.

24 *HC Deb.* 11 July 2001, col. 573–5w.

25 Thornton and Kirkup (2017)

26 *HC Deb.* 19 March 1963, col. 319.

27 Ingham 1991: 332.

Chapter 11

Ministerial responsibility: responsibility for what?

Ministers are answerable for their actions, formally to the crown, serving at the pleasure of the monarch, and politically to Parliament. They are answerable both individually and collectively. These responsibilities are variously accorded the status of conventions. However, as we noted in Chapter 3 in discussing collective responsibility, to describe it as a convention is problematic given that it comprises a set of rules, some of which are adhered to invariably and some of which are not; there is thus a mix of convention and practice. Some consistent behaviour derives largely from rules set for ministers, now embodied in a formal code, and therefore, even if followed invariably, does not qualify as a convention.

When we consider both individual and collective responsibility, there is a further problem. Collective responsibility may be invoked to protect a minister accused of breaching individual ministerial responsibility, ministers rallying round to protect one of their own.

This mix of rules, however problematic, is at the heart of the political system, determining the relationship between Parliament and the executive. It is necessary to ensure an accountable political system, ministers taking responsibility for their own actions, and with one body that stands before electors to take the blame or credit for public policy.

Individual responsibility

Ministers are deemed responsible for the policy and actions of their departments, but as Marshall and Moodie pointed out, 'responsibility' has a range of nuances.[1] It may refer to an action, indicate a relationship or function, or designate blame or praise. Referring instead to answerability encompasses similar problems, but may perhaps have a greater utility in terms of designating the minister as the public face of the department and speaking for it, be it to inform or to explain and accept (and act on) criticism.

The importance of individual ministerial responsibility lies primarily in establishing line management within a department. A senior minister is appointed to head a department. Civil servants answer to the minister, formally through the permanent secretary. The senior officials can identify options and advise, but at the end of the day it is the minister that decides. Civil servants then implement the decision. Although some departments have reputations for having a certain ethos or policy preference, they comply with ministerial directions. As the classic work of Bruce Headey revealed, civil servants like a minister who can take a view (that is, reach a decision).[2] 'Officials', as one former senior civil servant noted, 'need ministers with ideas ... Officials need stimulus; need leadership; and, on occasion, conflict'.[3] Ministers thus stand at the head of government departments, with not only officials, but also junior ministers answerable to them. When civil servants appear before select committees, they do so on behalf of their ministers. Similarly, in correspondence with parliamentarians and others, they write on behalf of their ministers. Individual ministerial responsibility thus establishes ministers as the pivot between departments and Parliament and indeed the wider environment. This is the most important and often overlooked consequence of individual ministerial responsibility, constituting, as Peter Richards observed, 'a major explanation for the isolation of Whitehall departments, for their inward-looking nature and for their constant emphasis on keeping within the policy bounds set from above'.[4] The advantage for officials is that they can speak freely within the department. The advantage for ministers is that information and advice has to flow up to them, without officials going public and arguing for their particular preferences.

'It is clear', wrote Richards in the 1980s, 'why ministers, who lose only a little and gain a great deal from the doctrine, should want to keep it going'.[5] However, the reality in recent years has been the increasing difficulty for ministers to keep abreast of what is going on in their departments. The size and complexity of departments, and the often technical aspects of major projects – which civil servants themselves may struggle to master – put pressure on the relationship between ministers and officials who answer to them, but who they are unable to remove. 'The tension between ministers and officials', reported the House of Commons Public Administration Committee, 'reflects that Whitehall is struggling to adapt to the demands of modern politics'.[6] The committee reported occasions when ministers felt that their officials were being obstructive.[7] In examining the case for civil service reform, it recognised that the civil service could not be seen in isolation, quoting the evidence of this writer that 'you cannot really produce a Civil Service that is fit for purpose unless you can do the same for ministers'.[8] Training of civil servants needed to be matched by training of ministers.[9] It recommended the creation of a parliamentary commission on the civil service to examine the long-term future of the service, a recommendation on which the government failed to act.

Despite the pressures on the relationship between ministers and their civil servants, the doctrine of individual ministerial responsibility provides the key framework governing their relationship. If anything, the pressures reinforce the importance of the doctrine. Without it, there would be blurred if almost non-existent lines of accountability to Parliament. As the Haldane Committee adumbrated, and as repeated in the *Cabinet Manual*, 'civil servants are accountable to ministers, who in turn are accountable to

Parliament'.[10] The doctrine, however imperfect or wilting, continues to shape the behaviour of ministers and their officials. It is the one unifying principle of government departments.

Ministers are the public face of their department. They answer for their policies and the actions of their departments, not least literally when at the despatch box to respond to questions and lead and respond to debates as well as when appearing before select committees. There is no legal requirement for ministers to appear in the chamber or before committees. Senior ministers may occasionally send a junior minister to respond to a debate or to give evidence to a select committee, even though they are not abroad or otherwise unavoidably detained. The attendance of senior ministers thus constitutes a practice rather than a convention. They do not regard themselves as morally obliged to appear on all occasions even when free to do so. Turning up to answer at question time is different in that attendance is seen as such an obligation.

The answerability of ministers is often seen in terms of culpability, ministers being expected to fall on their swords and resign in the event of some failing on their part or that of their departments. This, though, neither qualifies as a convention nor a practice. It has no basis in any consistent pattern of behaviour. The distinction is sometimes drawn between policy and operation. As former minister Nigel Forman observed, 'it has been effectively impossible for any senior Minister to be aware of, let alone control, everything which happens in his Department'.[11] In the event of administrative failure, the minister explains and takes corrective action. Where the failure is one of policy, the minister takes the blame and resigns. The distinction rarely bites in practice in that ministers are not prone to resign because of failures in their departments, be they the result of their own policy decisions or the actions of civil servants.

When ministers have resigned, they have done so, as we shall see, mostly for personal reasons (such as family or health) or because of scandals or, if over policy, because of disagreements with government policy, rather than for departmental failings.[12] Occasions when ministers have given up office because of failings associated with their departments are few and far between. In April 2018, Amber Rudd resigned as home secretary after she 'inadvertently misled' MPs over targets removing illegal immigrants. She had said there were no targets for removing such immigrants, but it then emerged there had been correspondence in the department showing that some targets had been set. Her resignation pales beside the number of resignations over government policy on leaving the European Union.

The case of Crichel Down in 1954 is seen as the classic case where a minister has taken the blame for the 'inefficiency and double-dealing' of civil servants and resigned.[13] However, it was more to do with ministerial policy than civil service behaviour. Although there was maladministration, and officials failed to inform the minister of some material information (and, following an investigation, some disciplinary action was taken), Agriculture Minister Sir Thomas Dugdale resigned because he had lost the confidence of his parliamentary party. The case involved land that had been purchased in 1937 for military use and after the war the original owners had not been given the opportunity to buy it back. The minister had concluded that it was appropriate to keep the land as one unit and to sell it to the commissioner for crown lands. This decision was unpopular with many Conservative MPs. Dugdale defended his action in a speech in the Commons, but announced a change of policy and concluded by announcing his resignation.[14] 'Now the 1922 Committee has the scalp of a Minister', declared Herbert Morrison from the opposition despatch box, 'and has a new policy in agriculture announced by the Minister at the point of his retirement'.[15]

This was an instance of a minister resigning because of their policy stance or actions losing the support of their party's MPs. There have been other such occasions, such as the foreign secretary,

Lord Carrington, resigning over policy towards the Falkland Islands in 1982 and Trade and Industry Secretary Leon Brittan resigning in 1986 over his role in the Westland affair. Both resigned after bruising meetings with the Conservative 1922 Committee.[16] However, again, such resignations are notable for being the exception rather than the rule. When under pressure over controversial actions, ministers have tended to stand firm and, so long as they retain the support of the prime minster and their parliamentary party, remain in office. They have not felt under a moral obligation to resign.

Resignations because of departmental failings are, then, exceptional, both relative to occasions when ministers have not resigned because of departmental failings and occasions when ministers have resigned, voluntarily or otherwise, because of personal scandals or disagreement with government policy.[17] The government of Theresa May saw resignations on an unprecedented scale, especially, though not exclusively, over the issue of Brexit. Between April 2018 and the end of September 2019, a total of thirty-eight ministers, including eleven cabinet ministers, resigned, though some media inflated the number to fifty by including parliamentary private secretaries. Of the thirty-eight, twenty-two resigned because of disagreements over Brexit policy, seven as a result of scandal, six for personal reasons (such as health) and three over other issues.

Individual ministers may thus come under significant pressure because of an unpopular policy or one that does not appear to be delivering what was expected of it, but as we have noted, will generally resist pressure to resign. They may draw on support from other ministers, who may rally round to support a colleague, not least because they do not wish to concede a scalp to political opponents. Major policies are also likely to have gone through cabinet committee, so ministers can draw on the collective strength of government in resisting pressure.

Individual ministerial responsibility should thus be seen primarily as imposing a duty to determine the policy of the department and answer to the House for that policy and the actions of the department. Insofar as it embodies a convention, it is in terms of answering for the department, but the physical manifestation of that is in appearing at the despatch box at question time. Actions beyond that come, at best, under the rubric of practice.

Collective responsibility

Ministers are held collectively responsible for the decisions of government and, as we noted in Chapter 3, once a policy is agreed by cabinet, they must support it publicly, both by voice and vote. Ministers are expected to speak freely in cabinet, but once a decision is reached, they must support it as well as maintain the confidentiality of their deliberations.

The emphasis is on achieving and maintaining a united front. The obligation developed over time, the impetus coming from the prime minister and monarch, and was a clear feature of government by the twentieth century. It is embodied now in the *Ministerial Code*: 'The principle of collective responsibility requires that Ministers should be able to express their views frankly in the expectation that they can argue freely in private while maintaining a united front when decisions have been reached. This in turn requires that the privacy of opinions expressed in Cabinet and Ministerial Committees … should be maintained.'[18] The essential point is that it comprises an obligation, one set in a code that ministers are required to abide by, unless the prime minister determines otherwise. If there is a breach, the prime minister may dismiss the minister or take, or decline to take, other disciplinary action. Ministers may feel some moral obligation to comply with the principle, but it rests on more than that. The sanction is external to the individual.

In an event, compliance is not invariable. As Keith put it, 'The theory is clear, but in practice there are relaxations'.[19] The obligation has tightened, but not quite to the extent of establishing invariable behaviour. The public perception of unity has not always matched the reality.

The need for collective responsibility has been recognised since the late eighteenth century. In 1792, prime minister William Pitt secured the dismissal of his lord chancellor after the latter launched an attack in the House of Lords on the prime minister's sinking fund, having raised no objections to it in council. This, wrote Harold Wilson, was 'the earliest known assertion of the principle of Cabinet collective responsibility'.[20]

The principle was extended in the nineteenth century to encompass all ministers, even though those outside the cabinet had not been party to the deliberations on the policy. Some junior ministers did on occasion vote against or fail to support the government, though in 1856 Queen Victoria told Lord Palmerston to make it clear 'to subordinate members of the Government that they cannot be allowed to vote against the Government proposal about the National Gallery tomorrow, as she hears that several fancy themselves at liberty to do so'.[21]

By the twentieth century, the obligation to support the government publicly by voice and vote was strong but, as expressed, did not quite match the reality. It would be more accurate to state that the requirement imposed on ministers was not to oppose, by voice or vote, decisions taken by the cabinet. The occasional discreet absence from a vote was tolerated.

In 1883 Sir Charles Dilke failed to vote against an amendment on female suffrage to the Reform Bill. Although reproved by Lord Hartington, he 'was not actually asked to resign, the matter being of minor importance'.[22] In 1948, the government took the view that ministers must accept collective responsibility on an amendment to the Criminal Justice Bill providing for a suspension of the death penalty for five years. Backbenchers were given a free vote, but government policy was to oppose it. However, given that some ministers held strong views on the issue, it was made known that they would be able to abstain, though not vote against the government line.[23] In 1975, one cabinet minister abstained on second reading of the Scotland and Wales Bill[24] and in 1978 an assistant whip abstained on second reading of the bill to increase the number of parliamentary seats in Northern Ireland.[25] In the 1980s, cabinet minister Jim Prior is believed to have abstained in at least one division.[26]

The principle has been undermined more corrosively in recent years by an erosion, or collapse, of the obligation of ministers to be loyal in voice to cabinet decisions and to vote with the government on government motions.

There is a history of cabinet ministers leaking information to favoured journalists, but for much of the twentieth century, even if secrecy was not maintained, at least there was no public division among ministers. In the 1960s, some ministers, Prime Minister Harold Wilson recorded, 'apparently felt free… to dissociate themselves from certain of the Government's policies and to allow this to be made known to outside bodies'.[27] Wilson was particularly upset at Home Secretary James Callaghan, who was a member of Labour's National Executive Committee (NEC), using his position on the NEC to oppose the government's policy on industrial relations. Callaghan conceded in his memoirs that during 1968 and 1969 he was 'for part of that period … at odds semi-publicly with the Prime Minister about Barbara Castle's proposals for handling industrial relations in response to a plague of unofficial strikes'.[28] Despite Wilson's attempts to put an end to such leaking, ministers since have variously let their disagreement with policies find its way into the public domain. The extent to which media report cabinet divisions, identifying at times the ministers expressing dissent, suggests that some ministers have no compunction about phoning a friendly journalist to put their side of an argument. Jack Straw, who served in cabinet from 1997 to 2010, complained about briefings being given to the press when they should have been made first to Parliament. 'Equally often', he recalled, 'such stories leaked out through incontinence by ambitious ministers or their special advisers'.[29]

Such incontinence has become a well-established feature of contemporary political life, notable not least as a result of conflict over Brexit. 'Cabinet became steadily more leaky from early 2018 onwards ... Stories of leaking were legend ... [Liam] Fox says he'd never seen anything like it in twenty-seven years in politics'.[30] One senior official was quoted as saying 'It became pointless for the Prime Minister to start a meeting with the words "please stop leaking" because it made no difference, it merely diminished her authority'.[31] Cabinet confidentiality was maintained more in the breach than the observance.

However, the obligation not to speak on a public platform or vote against the government was enforced, unless the prime minister decided otherwise.

There were three occasions in the twentieth century when the principle was suspended by the prime minister to enable ministers to take different sides in an argument. These were in 1932 on tariff protection, in 1975 on the European Communities referendum, and in 1977 on second reading of the European Assembly Elections Bill.[32] It was also suspended under the coalition government of David Cameron to allow ministers to argue on different sides primarily in the 2011 referendum on electoral reform, and – at very short notice and on the decision not of the prime minister, but the deputy prime minister, Nick Clegg – in 2012 when Liberal Democrat ministers voted against the government on constituency boundary revisions. In short, the obligation was in the ownership of the premier (or, in coalition, premier or deputy premier), not in the consciences of individual ministers.

The requirement not to vote against the government where the premier did not suspend collective responsibility was, though, seriously challenged under the premiership of Theresa May. Ministers defied the government position in some divisions on Brexit. In March 2019, thirteen ministers, including four cabinet ministers, were allowed by Downing Street to abstain on a motion ruling out a no-deal Brexit in all circumstances. (One of the ministers did choose then to resign; the rest remained in post.) Although, as we have seen, a minister has occasionally been permitted to be discreetly absent before, this was very public abstention on a substantial scale and extensively reported in the media. One Conservative MP declared: 'The collective responsibility has disintegrated – you might as well tell the whips to pack up and go home. The government is barely in office.'[33]

However, what was most remarkable was what occurred on 14 March, when eight cabinet ministers, including the Brexit secretary, voted against the government motion supporting an extension under article 50,[34] even though the Brexit secretary had wound up the debate on behalf of the government. After the vote, the prime minister's spokesperson 'said it was clear it was a free vote on Thursday night but that cabinet ministers who voted against the government motion would now be expected to follow government policy'.[35] It appeared to be a case of asserting that it was a free vote after becoming apparent that the prime minister, in a weak political position, would not be able to get her ministers to vote for the motion. Given the number of ministers she had already lost over the issue of Brexit, she could not then afford to lose a third of her cabinet.

Her successor, Boris Johnson, was in a stronger position, having just been elected as party leader, and so the obligation to support the government was resuscitated and remains a feature of British government. Collective responsibility, as we have seen, is embodied in the *Ministerial Code*, the latest version published in August 2019, stipulating what is expected of ministers. Ministers may feel a moral obligation to support the government of which they are members and in any event are, other than in exceptional circumstances, going to be in agreement with it. However, they are required by a third party (the prime minister) to adhere to it under threat of dismissal if they do not. The prime minister may also qualify its application. As Prime Minister James Callaghan put it in 1977, 'I certainly think that the doctrine should apply, except in cases where I announce that it does not'.[36] It thus may be deemed to constitute a rule imposed on ministers, rather than one deriving exclusively from their sense of right behaviour. As Labour MP Brian Sedgemore once observed, 'the doctrine is not without virtue. But no doctrine can ever be absolute'.[37]

Conclusion

Ministerial responsibility, both individual and collective, has come under increasing strain in recent years. Some of the pressures derive from longer-term changes in the nature of government (size, complexity, large-scale procurement and the creation of executive agencies) and others more recent, not least as a result of Brexit. Yet ministerial responsibility constitutes the defining feature at the heart not only of relations between ministers and civil servants, but also between government and Parliament. It determines not only who answers to Parliament for what goes on in departments, but also ensures there is one clear entity – the government – that stands before Parliament and accepts responsibility for public policy. Government rests on the confidence of the House of Commons in between elections and stands before electors at election time to accept blame or praise for its policies and conduct of the nation's affairs. The doctrine underpins the accountability at the heart of the British constitution. Without it, there is no one entity that electors can hold to account for public policy.

> The principle [of collective responsibility] is not consistently observed or enforced in a strict sense, and has on occasion been suspended in relation to particular issues. Nevertheless, despite quite frequent minor breaches, occasional major defiance, and different degrees of observance between one administration and another, the principle does express in a general way the actual practice of government.[38]

Notes

1   Marshall and Moodie 1967: 58.
2   Headey 1974.
3   Holland 1995: 43.
4   Richards 1984: 181.
5   Richards 1984: 182.
6   Public Administration Committee, House of Commons 2013: 9.
7   Public Administration Committee, House of Commons 2013: 23–4.
8   Public Administration Committee, House of Commons 2013: 50.
9   Lord Norton, in Public Administration Committee, House of Commons 2013: ev251–4.
10   Cabinet Office 2011: 57.
11   Forman 1991: 196.
12   See Norton 2018b: 473.
13   Harvey and Bather 1963: 297–8.
14   *HC Deb.* 20 July 1954, cols. 1178–94.
15   *HC Deb.* 20 July 1954, col. 1283.
16   Norton 2013e: 71.
17   Norton 2018b: 473.
18   Cabinet Office 2019: 4.
19   Keith 1952: 93.
20   Wilson 1977: 30; see also Blake 1975: 30–1.
21   Keith 1952: 97.
22   Keith 1952: 95.
23   Keith 1952: 97.
24   Norton 1982: 64.
25   Norton 1989: 35.
26   Norton 1989: 34.
27   Wilson 1977: 232.
28   Callaghan 1988: 272.
29   Straw 2012: 242.
30   Seldon 2019: 377–8.
31   Seldon 2019: 378.
32   Norton 1982: 64.
33   *PoliticsHome*, 13 March 2019.
34   *HC Deb.* 14 March 2019, cols. 647–51.
35   *Guardian*, 14 March 2019.
36   *HC Deb.* 16 June 1977, col. 552.
37   Sedgemore 1980: 75.
38   Turpin 1985: 73.

Chapter 12

Devolution: a disunited union?

The United Kingdom is a unitary state. The doctrine of parliamentary sovereignty ensures that nobody is outwith the writ of the crown-in-Parliament (Chapter 1). Parliament may create different bodies with authority to generate enforceable rules within a specified jurisdiction, but that power is granted by Parliament and may be removed by Parliament.

Parliament has created different layers of local government and has variously changed the configuration and powers of that government. More recently, it has legislated to create elected bodies with legislative and/or executive powers in three of the four nations within the United Kingdom. It has also provided for some decentralisation of government within England. Changes have ranged from giving some powers to a mayor and assembly in London to powers conferred on cities or city regions, but with other parts of England left without a regional 'power house'.

The devolution or disbursement of powers from the centre to national and regional levels has been a notable feature of the period since the end of the twentieth century. There are various models that have been generated to help make sense of the changing distribution of power within the UK.[1] One is federalism – dual or co-operative – power being shared between the different levels of government.[2] Another is European regionalism, with regions relying less than before on the nation state and dealing with the

EU directly. A third has been akin to a Commonwealth solution, nations moving to self-determination and independence. There is not necessarily a strong link between theory and the practice, change resulting from conflicting pressures rather than agreement on what form of power distribution is appropriate for the United Kingdom. Insofar as political parties favour any of the models, the preferences differ between the parties, with some embracing positions that constitute existentialist threats to the union of the United Kingdom.

As such, devolution reflects the situation with the UK constitution generally. That is, there have been and continue to be significant changes, on a scale not seen for centuries, but without those changes deriving from a coherent view of what system of government is deemed appropriate for the United Kingdom. Change has, in effect, been bottom-up rather than top-down, deriving from pressures that differ in extent and form. The result is a patchwork quilt of law-making public bodies in the United Kingdom.

The change also reflects the situation similar to the UK's relation with the European Union. There has never been a settled period. In relation to the EU, the UK has always been in in a position of playing catch-up, of trying to make sense of the constitutional consequences of different treaties negotiated since membership. The same applies to devolution. The Welsh Secretary in 1997, Ron Davies, described devolution as 'a process, not an event'. References to a 'devolution settlement' are effectively aspirational rather than descriptive. The relationship between the centre and elected bodies in different parts of the UK has been one of flux since powers were devolved. There has never been a settled state.

The UK general election of 2019 produced a decisive political outcome, but added to the constitutional pressures of devolution. A Conservative government, committed to the union of the United Kingdom, achieved a decisive majority, producing some settlement at Westminster, but two parts of the United Kingdom (Scotland and Northern Ireland) each returned a majority of MPs from nationalist parties. The SNP, with forty-eight out of the fifty-nine MPs returned from Scotland, claimed a mandate for a second referendum on independence in the face of a government opposed to one.

There is no clear solution to what amounts to a constitutional conundrum. Political parties that dominate in each part of the UK espouse constitutional goals that are mutually exclusive.

Scotland and Wales

The twentieth century witnessed growing demands in Scotland, and to a lesser extent, Wales, for independence or at least for each to have its own parliament, in the case of Scotland to have one again. There was resistance to what was seen as overly centralised decision-making in London, with calls for decision-making to be made closer to the people.[3] The royal commission on the constitution (the Kilbrandon commission) that reported in 1973, recommended some devolution of powers, with elected assemblies in Scotland and Wales.

The principle underpinning devolution has been consistent – devolving powers closer to people so that they can have a say in what affects their particular area. The benefits are deemed to be twofold, political (giving people a greater sense of attachment to the process) and economic (greater efficiency through targeting resources where needed).[4] In the 1970s, as pressure for devolution to Scotland and Wales increased, the Labour government and Plaid Cymru in Wales tended to stress the political imperative, while the SNP was more active in emphasising the economic.[5] The principled case was variously challenged, but the tipping point in favour of Labour governments embracing devolution for Scotland, Wales and, indeed, Northern Ireland, was political. Labour had established itself as the dominant party in Scotland and was keen to see off the growing challenge from the SNP. Economic decline and the discovery of oil in the North Sea fuelled support for independence.[6] The fact that Scotland retained its own legal and educational system, and was administrated as a distinct entity through the Scottish Office, meant that it already had a recognisable measure of administrative integrity.

The decades since the 1970s have seen attempts, ultimately successful, to devolve powers to elected bodies in Scotland and Wales. Initial attempts under the Labour government of 1974–9 failed after the House of Commons, against the government's wishes, insisted on devolution being subject to confirmation by referendum with a threshold requirement. Wales voted overwhelmingly against devolution. There was a narrow majority in Scotland voting 'yes', but not sufficient to meet the threshold of 40 per cent of registered voters casting their votes in favour. Conservative governments from 1979 onwards opposed devolution. It was not until the Blair government of 1997 that devolution legislation was enacted, with Scotland getting a parliament with legislative and executive powers and Wales a national assembly with executive powers. The Scottish Parliament was empowered to legislate in all areas, other than those reserved to Westminster, primarily foreign and defence policy, fiscal matters and social security policy.

The creation of both bodies failed to still demands for further devolution or independence, in Scotland especially. Devolution has not delivered on its intended political consequences. As Aileen McHarg has observed, 'The electoral system for the Scottish Parliament was designed deliberately to avoid single-party majority governments'.[7] In this, it failed. Far from devolution seeing off the challenge to Labour from the SNP, the SNP has become the 'in' party of Scottish government, forming the government of Scotland since 2007 and, for one Parliament (2011–16), winning an outright majority. It has thus been in power for most of the existence of the Scottish Parliament. In the UK general election of 2015, it achieved almost a clean sweep of Scottish constituencies, winning fifty-six of the fifty-nine seats. It has pressed the case for independence, deploying the arguments used initially for devolution: countering a democratic deficit and more effective governance[8] and making much of the running in debate.

The response of succeeding UK governments has been to concede a further devolution of powers. Under the Government of Wales Act 2006, a process of transferring legislative powers to the national assembly began. Following a referendum in March 2011, provided for under the act, the sixty-member assembly was empowered to legislate in devolved matters without the need for Westminster approval. Following the report of a commission (the Calman commission), further powers were given to Scotland under the Scotland Act 2012. Foremost among these was the ability to raise or lower income tax by up to 10p in the pound and to give the Scottish government the power to borrow money up to £5 billion.

Under pressure from the SNP government, the coalition government in 2014 conceded the case for a referendum on independence. All three main party leaders at Westminster committed to further devolution if electors voted no. The referendum produced a 54–46 per cent vote for staying in the union. The government then delivered on its commitment and, following recommendations of a commission under Lord Smith of Kelvin,[9] enacted the Scotland Act 2016, providing for the transfer of further powers. These included the power to amend provisions of the 1998 Scotland Act relating to the operation of the parliament and government, including the capacity to control its electoral system, as well as transfer powers in areas covering onshore oil and gas activity, energy efficiency, and rail franchising. It gave substantial control over income tax, not least in respect of income tax rates on non-savings and non-dividend income. In Wales, also after a report from a commission (the Silk commission), the Wales Act 2017 provided for a reserved powers model, with all powers devolved unless specifically reserved under the act to Westminster.

Devolution has also given rise to dissatisfaction in England – the 'English question' – at the perceived benefits being conferred, both political (the West Lothian question) and economic (the Barnett formula), on Scotland.[10] The West Lothian question was not new – it had arisen in the 1880s in debate on the Irish home rule bill.[11] It revolved around the position of MPs returned to Westminster from that part of the UK granted home rule. Should those MPs be allowed to vote on issues at Westminster that affected only England, given that MPs from English constituencies could not vote on the equivalent issue affecting the devolved nation?[12] The Barnett formula is a non-statutory process, devised in 1977–8 by chief secretary to the Treasury, Joel Barnett, to determine the allocation of funds under the annual block grant. If there is a change in a government department's spending, the formula then takes into account the percentage of comparable services in the devolved area and the population in the area. The formula has been criticised for benefiting Scotland. In 2007–8, expenditure per head in England was £1,600 less than in Scotland.[13]

In terms of political representation, the Labour government conceded the case for doing what had been included in the home rule bill in 1893 and undertaken in 1922 when Northern Ireland gained a parliament. That was to reduce the number of MPs sent to Westminster from the devolved area below the number that its population would otherwise justify. As a result, the number of MPs returned from Scotland to Westminster was reduced from seventy-two to fifty-nine with effect from the 2005 general election. Conversely, after the Stormont parliament was abolished, the number of MPs returned from Northern Ireland was increased. However, no change was made following the Good Friday Agreement and the creation of a Northern Ireland assembly.

The reduction in the number of seats for Scotland did not dissipate resentment in England[14] and, as a response to the English question, the Conservative Party embraced English votes for English laws (EVEL). The means of delivering this has been to provide that only MPs from English constituencies can vote on legislative provisions dealing exclusively with England. In the event, the system introduced has not been so much to provide for English votes *for* English laws as to provide for an English *veto* over English laws.

The result has been not only a patchwork quilt of government in the UK, but also a complicated process for dealing with legislation in the House of Commons. Rather than legislating for EVEL, the 2015 Conservative government sought to deliver it through amending the standing orders of the House. Provisions of a bill certified by the Speaker as relating exclusively to England are referred for an extra stage involving only MPs from English (or English and Welsh) constituencies. A measure agreed by the House is thus subject to further approval. The process is so complex that few MPs understand it and, perhaps more significantly, as Gover and Kenny have shown, it has not proved effective in giving either a distinctive English voice or a veto in the legislative process.[15] The Barnett formula remains in place, not so much on grounds of principle, but because it is the default position until an alternative that is both practical and politically acceptable has been found. A House of Lords select committee argued for its replacement – Joel (Lord) Barnett was among those arguing against it – but none is in sight.[16]

As is clear from the foregoing, the policies pursued by successive UK governments have been responsive, introducing measures to address demands for greater powers from different parts of the United Kingdom and to meet the dissatisfaction expressed in England. The positive case for the union[17] has not been to the fore. The House of Lords Consitution Committee in a report in 2016 on *The Union and Devolution*, drew attention to the ad hoc way in which power has been devolved. 'Every system has its limits', it recorded. 'This haphazard approach to the UK's constitution, in which power has been devolved without any counter-balancing steps to protect the Union, recently culminated in an existentialist threat in the form of a referendum on Scottish independence. An inattentive approach to the integrity of the Union cannot continue.'[18] Subsequent events, as we shall see, have created further pressures without a coherent approach to the future of the union being developed.

Northern Ireland

The fact that Northern Ireland requires to be considered separately from Scotland and Wales reflects the disparate and discrete nature of devolution in the United Kingdom.

Irish home rule was the dominant issue of British politics in the late nineteenth and early twentieth centuries. It was divisive and, like Brexit in the twenty-first century, led politicians to prioritise desired policy outcomes over the principles of the constitution. In the event, Ireland gained independence, but the northern counties remained part of the United Kingdom. The province was given home rule, with its own parliament and government at Stormont. The parliament existed for fifty years, largely left to its own devices and neglected at Westminster.[19] It constituted an era of 'dual politics',[20] with Northern Ireland effectively operating, as O'Leary and McGarry characterised it, as a semi-state.[21] Leaving it to look after itself proved part of the problem in that the centre neglected the way the province was governed. The nationalist minority resented the discriminatory policies of the Unionist government and protested, leading to clashes and also armed conflict.

The result was 'the troubles' and the suspension in 1972 and then abolition of the parliament after the Stormont government resisted attempts by the UK government to assume responsibility for law and order in the province and to find a political settlement for the conflict. Direct rule from Whitehall was introduced. Attempts at creating a power-sharing executive in the 1970s and 1980s stumbled and failed. Some progress was made between the UK and Irish governments in the 1985 Anglo-Irish agreement, recognising the right of the province to self-determination and establishing an intergovernmental conference, but it was opposed by Unionist parties in the province.

The following decade, however, saw a political breakthrough and negotiations leading to an agreement – the Belfast, or Good Friday, agreement – in 1998. It embodied two agreements, one between the UK and Eire (the British–Irish agreement), and the other (formally an annex to the first) between the two governments and most of the political parties in Northern Ireland (the multi-party agreement). They established that Northern Ireland was part of the UK and would stay so until a majority of the people in Northern Ireland and the Republic of Ireland decided otherwise. The UK repealed its claim to the territory of Ireland (which had been included in the Government of Ireland Act 1920) and the Republic withdrew its territorial claim to Northern Ireland. The agreement also established institutions both within Northern Ireland (assembly and power-sharing executive), between the north and south (ministerial council, inter-parliamentary association, consultative forum) and between the east and west, that is, the two nations (a British–Irish intergovernmental conference, council and inter-parliamentary body). It also committed the UK government to enshrining the ECHR into law as well as recognising both governments as 'partners in the European Union'.

The nature of the agreements not only created a situation that was constitutionally novel, but so too did the means by which it was given democratic, and not just legal, confirmation. There were referendums in both the north and the south, the former to approve the multi-party agreement and the latter to agree changes to the Irish constitution necessitated by the agreement. There were overwhelming 'yes' votes in each (71 per cent in Northern Ireland, 94 per cent in the Republic). This created what amounted in effect to a double-lock, since it would be difficult to undo the agreement without referendums on both sides of the border.

The Northern Ireland Act 1998 provided for devolution in Northern Ireland in line with the agreement as well as providing that the province would not cease to be part of the UK without the consent of a majority of its people. It also enshrined principles embodied in the agreement, including a prohibition on discrimination on grounds of religious belief or political opinion and the imposition of equality duties on government departments and public bodies. Not dissimilar to other devolution legislation, it confirmed the doctrine of parliamentary sovereignty, stating that nothing prevented Westminster from legislating for Northern Ireland. It differed from other devolution legislation, though, in creating three, rather than two, types of legislative competence – transferred, reserved and excepted matters. The Northern Ireland assembly was empowered to legislate in 'transferred matters', in effect areas not reserved to Westminster. Powers that remain with Westminster comprise those that can never be transferred ('excepted matters') and those that may at some stage be transferred ('reserved matters').

The form of government created for Northern Ireland is thus *sui generis*. It is part of a distinctive constitutional framework, distinguishable from that created for other parts of the United Kingdom. Executive positions are allocated to parties on a formula basis, with the first and deputy first minister each having independent powers and with the involvement of the two largest parties being necessary for the executive to operate.

The two largest parties in the first power-sharing executive, formed in 1999, were the Ulster Unionist Party (UUP) and the Social and Democratic and Labour Party (SDLP). Devolution was variously suspended because of conflicts, most notably in 2002 when the UUP refused to share power with the Sinn Fein party after an investigation into an alleged Provisional IRA spy ring. The 2002 suspension lasted until 2007 when, somewhat counterintuitively, the two parties seen at the political extremes in the province – the DUP and Sinn Féin, which had eclipsed the UUP and

SDLP respectively in popular support – agreed to co-operate in the executive. The executive lasted until January 2017, when it collapsed following a scandal over a renewable heat incentive scheme.

The province was then administered in effect by the Northern Irish civil service and in 2019 the UK Parliament enacted the Northern Ireland (Executive Formation and Exercise of Functions) Act to keep services operating. Conditions changed following the 2019 general election, in which both Sinn Féin and the DUP lost support, the main beneficiaries being the SDLP and Alliance Party. The result acted as a spur to entering negotiations and in January 2020 agreement was reached and a new power-sharing executive, drawn from five parties, was formed and the assembly resumed sitting. According to former Sinn Féin president Gerry Adams, previously derided as a terrorist by Unionists, the assembly provided a place to 'moderate differences, and to define common ground'.[22]

The nature of government in the province has thus been distinctive and problematic.[23] However, the existence of a DUP–Sinn Féin government for a decade was an achievement. Despite still demonstrating divisions within the province, with religion creating a communal divide, 'twenty years of the Belfast Agreement have resulted in the broad contours emerging of an internal political settlement within Northern Ireland'.[24] From 2007 to 2017, as Haughey has recorded, the assembly enacted more primary legislation than any other devolved legislature.[25] A culture of co-operation and collaboration developed between its committees.[26] Paramilitary violence in the province has largely disappeared, with parties committed to a united Ireland fighting for their goals through the ballot box.

Brexit and devolution

Brexit has significant consequences for the union. There are problems deriving not only from disagreement on the merits of

Brexit, but also on intergovernmental relations as a consequence of Brexit. In the 2016 referendum, Scotland and Northern Ireland recorded majority votes to remain in the EU. Although the DUP supported Brexit, in 2019 it swung against the UK government's withdrawal agreement, viewing it as undermining the integrity of the province. The SNP wanted an independent Scotland to be in the EU. Brexit was thus seen as exacerbating the possible break-up of the union.

Discussions over the terms of withdrawal from the EU also increased tensions between the UK government and the Scottish and Welsh executives. The stance of the UK government in its approach to policy competences reverting from the EU to the UK met opposition. The government of Theresa May favoured powers, which otherwise would flow to the devolved legislatures, being retained at UK level until the government decided what to do with them. Although some compromises were agreed between the UK, Scottish and Welsh executives to the Withdrawal Agreement Bill 2018, the measure was passed without the consent of the Scottish Parliament. As a result, the Scottish government went on a 'Sewel strike', refusing in most cases to seek consent motions for UK-wide Brexit legislation.

Although some concessions were achieved in areas of joint interest, not least in the creation of what amounted to a joint ministerial committee on trade, little progress was made in a review of intergovernmental relations commissioned at the start of 2018 by the prime ministers and first ministers. Both the Scottish and UK governments had tended to rely on an informal style of communication[27] at the expense of the machinery created when devolution was introduced. As the Welsh Brexit minister, Jeremy Miles, observed in 2019, what progress that had been made was patchy. 'And even where relations are positive and constructive, they rely far too heavily on individual relationships.'[28] No progress had been made, he noted, in the devolved governments' calls to form a council of ministers and a better system for dispute resolution. The inadequacies of the means for dispute resolution were longstanding. As far back as 2003, the House of Lords Constitution Committee had identified the need for the machinery for dispute resolution – the joint ministerial council – to be kept in good working order.[29]

At the heart of the problems encountered by the May government in 2019 in seeking parliamentary approval for the withdrawal agreement was opposition to the so-called 'Northern Irish backstop'. Under this, the whole of the UK would remain in effect within the EU until the problem of the border with Ireland was resolved. This provision proved unacceptable to a large number of Conservative MPs, who joined with the opposition to impose the biggest government defeat in modern British history. It led to the resignation of the prime minister and the negotiation, under the new prime minister, Boris Johnson, of a protocol on Northern Ireland. This avoided the need for a 'hard' border between Northern Ireland and the Republic, but without clarity as to the precise means for giving effect to the protocol.

The 2019 general election gave the new prime minister the majority he needed to get the withdrawal agreement approved by Parliament and for the UK to exit the European Union on 31 January 2020. Leaving the EU still left open the issue of how the agreement on Northern Ireland would work in practice. It also left unresolved the impact on the Good Friday Agreement and the peace process. It failed to resolve the tensions between the UK government and the devolved administrations. These were likely to be marked in terms of trade negotiations which, although falling within the reserved category, had major consequences for the different parts of the UK. There was, as Jeremy Miles noted, the attitude of the UK government to devolution, adopting a 'grace and favour' approach, rather than one of mutual esteem and participation. Brexit, he argued, would add to the existing tensions that characterised the constitutional architecture of the United Kingdom.

Conclusion

The potential for constitutional conflict between England and Scotland has been inherent since the time of the Act of Union. As the Kilbrandon commission noted, proposals for the union 'were controversial at the time and … the consequences of the Union have since been the subject of much heated debate in Scotland'.[30]

The union of two nations was treated in effect as Scotland being added to and absorbed by England, certainly in terms of parliament and the doctrine of parliamentary sovereignty. This has never been fully conceded by the Scottish courts. As Lord President Cooper observed in his *obiter dictum* in *MacCormick* v. *Lord Advocate* in 1953, 'The principle of the unlimited sovereignty of Parliament is a distinctively English principle which has no counterpart in Scottish constitutional law'.[31] The basis on which the UK government ensures its policies apply throughout the UK is contested rather than willingly conceded north of the border.

Devolution and Brexit have added to, rather than dissipated, tensions within the union. Successive governments have sought to address the pressures more on an individual rather than holistic basis, responding to demands rather than articulating and implementing a coherent constitutional settlement. Constitutionally, there is both conflict (independence versus maintaining the union) and confusion, with a patchwork quilt of government and at times near cavalier approach by the UK government to the constitution.

Various solutions offered to resolve the constitutional tensions include a codified constitution (see Chapter 1) and, as an alternative, the passage of a Constitutional Reform Act. The act, argues Brice Dickson, should provide for a UK federation and include a purpose clause 'setting out the clear goals which the United Kingdom seeks to achieve as a nation'.[32] It should also embody a replacement for the Barnett formula. The problem here is reaching agreement on the goals that the United Kingdom seeks to achieve. As the House of Lords Constitution Committee argued in its 2016 report, the case for the union has largely gone unheard. As the situation stands, the sum of the parts of the United Kingdom is in danger of being greater than the whole.

The UK government has yet to take both a proactive and holistic approach to the union, a reactive approach serving more as a sticking plaster than a healing tonic. At a practical level, the Barnett formula has few friends, but achieving agreement on an alternative is problematic. Meeting English criticisms will fuel SNP demands for independence. A holistic approach necessitates a clear grasp of the constitutional pressures at work and recognition that the future of the United Kingdom may rest on adopting an intergovernmental, or dualist, approach rather than one of supremacy. Brexit provides an impetus for a review and, as such, constitutes an opportunity as well as a threat. As the Institute for Government argued in its 2018 report, *Devolution after Brexit*: 'Brexit will require the UK and the devolved nations to co-operate actively in a way that has not always been necessary within the EU structures. The four nations should seize this chance to strengthen their relationship.'[33]

As Nicola McEwen succinctly put it, 'The United Kingdom … faces a constitutional crossroads, and the direction of travel remains unclear'.[34] If a traffic light system were to be employed for the constitutional pressures facing the union, it would likely be on an amber alert. How the UK government and devolved administrations interact will determine whether it moves more towards red or green.

Notes

1   Todd 2005; see also Deacon 2018.
2   McEwen 2016: 228–9.
3   See e.g. Birch 1977; Jefferson 2011.
4   Norton 1982: 181.
5   Norton 1982: 182.
6   Birch 1977; Drucker and Brown 1980.

7   McHarg 2016: 101.

8   McHarg 2016: 104–15.

9   See Kenealy *et al.* 2017: ch. 4.

10   See Hazell 2006; Jeffrey *et al.* 2016.

11   Norton 2011b: 177–9.

12   Dalyell 2016: 90–1.

13   Select Committee on the Barnett Formula 2009: evidence 1.

14   Norton 2011b: 185–8.

15   Gover and Kenny 2018: 760–82.

16   Select Committee on the Barnett Formula 2009.

17   See Gallagher 2016: 127–52.

18   Constitution Committee, House of Lords 2016: 3.

19   Norton 1996c: 129–31.

20   Bulpitt 1983.

21   O'Leary and McGarry 1990: 11.

22   BBC News Online, 12 January 2020.

23   Nagle 2018: 395–416; Shirlow 2018: 392–4.

24   Teague 2019: 692.

25   Haughey 2019: 706.

26   Haughey 2019: 706–7.

27   Cairney 2011: 85–115.

28   Speech at the Wales Governance Centre, 17 June 2019.

29   Constitution Committee, House of Lords 2003: 5, 15–18.

30   Royal Commission on the Constitution 1973: 22.

31   See Norton 2011b: 176.

32   Dickson 2019: 101.

33   Thimont Jack *et al.* 2018: 4.

34   McEwen 2016: 240.

References

Adams, R. J. Q. (1999), *Bonar Law*, London: John Murray.

Amery, L. S. (1953), *Thoughts on the Constitution*, 2nd edn, Oxford: Oxford University Press.

Aroney, N. (2015), 'Law and Convention', in B. Galligan and S. Brenton (eds), *Constitutional Conventions in Westminster Systems*, Cambridge: Cambridge University Press.

Bagehot, W. (1963), *The English Constitution* (first pub. 1867), London: Fontana.

Barber, N. W. (2018), *The Principles of Constitutionalism*, Oxford: Oxford University Press.

Barry, N., Miragliotta, N. and Nwokora, Z. (2019), 'The Dynamics of Constitutional Conventions in Western Democracies', *Parliamentary Affairs*, Vol. 72 (3).

BBC News Online (2019), 'Supreme Court: Suspending Parliament was unlawful, judges rule', 24 September. https://www.bbc.co.uk/news/uk-politics-49810261 accessed 25 March 2020.

Bingham, T. (2010), *The Rule of Law*, London: Allen Lane.

Birch, A. H. (1964), *Representative and Responsible Government*, London: George Allen & Unwin.

Birch, A. H. (1977), *Political Integration and Disintegration in the British Isles*, London: Allen & Unwin.

Birkinshaw, P. (2003), *European Public Law*, London: Butterworths.

Blair, T. (2010), *A Journey*, London: Hutchinson.

Blair, T. (2019), 'A simple referendum will solve Brexit – not a chaotic general election', *Evening Standard*, 6 September.

Blake, R. (1955), *The Unknown Prime Minister*, London: Eyre & Spottiswoode.

Blake, R. (1975), *The Office of Prime Minister*, Oxford: Oxford University Press.

Blake R. (1993), 'How Churchill Became Prime Minister', in R. Blake and W. R. Louis (eds), *Churchill*, Oxford: Oxford University Press.

183

References

Blick, A. (2015), *Beyond Magna Carta: A Constitution for the United Kingdom*, Oxford: Hart Publishing.

Bogdanor, V. (1995), *The Monarchy and the Constitution*, Oxford: Clarendon Press.

Bogdanor, V. (1997), *Power and the People*, London: Victor Gollancz.

Bogdanor, V. (2009), *The New British Constitution*, Oxford: Hart Publishing.

Bogdanor, V. (2019), *Beyond Brexit: Towards a British Constitution*, London: I. B. Tauris.

Bradley, A. W., Ewing, K. D. and Knight, C. J. S. (2015), *Constitutional and Administrative Law*, 16th edn, Harlow: Pearson.

Brazier, R. (2008), *Constitutional Reform*, 3rd edn, Oxford: Oxford University Press.

Brown, G. (1972), *In My Way*, Harmondsworth: Penguin.

Bulpitt, J. (1983), *Territory and Power in the United Kingdom*, Manchester: Manchester University Press.

Butler, D. and Kitzinger, U. (1976), *The 1975 Referendum*, London: Macmillan.

Butler, D. and Ranney, A. (1994), *Referendums Around the World*, updated edn, Washington, DC: American Enterprise Institute.

Butler, Lord (1973), *The Art of the Possible*, Harmondsworth: Penguin.

Cabinet Office (2011), *The Cabinet Manual*, London: Cabinet Office.

Cabinet Office (2019), *Ministerial Code*, London: Cabinet Office.

Cairney, P. (2011), *The Scottish Political System Since Devolution*, Exeter: Imprint Academic.

Callaghan, J. (1988), *Time & Change*, London: Fontana.

Castiglione, D. (1996), 'The Political Theory of the Constitution', in R. Bellamy and D. Castiglione (eds), *Constitutionalism in Transformation: European and Theoretical Perspectives*, Oxford: Blackwell.

Castle, B. (1980), *The Castle Diaries 1974–76*, London: Weidenfeld & Nicolson.

Cini, M. (2003), 'Intergovernmentalism', in M. Cini (ed.), *European Union Politics*, Oxford: Oxford University Press.

Clarke, H., Goodwin, M. and Whiteley, P. (2017), *Brexit: Why Britain Voted to Leave the European Union*, Cambridge: Cambridge University Press.

Committee of Privileges, House of Commons (2019), *Conduct of Mr Dominic Cummings*, First Report, Session 2017–19, HC 1490, London: The Stationery Office.

Conservative Party (2019), *Get Brexit Done: Unleash Britain's Potential. The Conservative and Unionist Manifesto 2019*, London: Conservative & Unionist Party.

Constitution Committee, House of Lords (2003), *Devolution: Inter-Institutional Relations in the United Kingdom*, 2nd Report, Session 2002–03, HL Paper 28, London: The Stationery Office.

Constitution Committee, House of Lords (2010a), *Referendums in the United Kingdom*, 12th Report, Session 2009–10, HL Paper 99, London: The Stationery Office.

References

Constitution Committee, House of Lords (2010b), *Fixed-Term Parliaments Bill*, 8th Report, Session 2010–11, HL Paper 69, London: The Stationery Office.

Constitution Committee, House of Lords (2014), *Constitutional Arrangements for the Use of Armed Force*, 2nd Report, Session 2013–14, HL Paper 46, London: The Stationery Office.

Constitution Committee, House of Lords (2016), *The Union and Devolution*, 10th Report, Session 2015–16, HL Paper 149, London: The Stationery Office.

Constitution Committee, House of Lords (2019), *Parliamentary Scrutiny of Treaties*, 20th Report, Session 2017–19, HL Paper 345, London: The Stationery Office.

Constitution Unit (2018), *Report of the Independent Commission on Referendums*, London: University College London Constitution Unit.

Corstens, G. (2017), *Understanding the Rule of Law*, Oxford: Hart Publishing.

Craig, P. (2018), '*Miller*, EU Law and the UK', in M. Elliott, J. Williams and A. L. Young (eds), *The UK Constitution after Miller*, Oxford: Hart Publishing.

Dahl, R. A. (1966), 'Some Explanations', in R. A. Dahl (ed.), *Political Opposition in Western Democracies*, New Haven: Yale University Press.

Dalyell, T. (2016), *The Question of Scotland: Devolution and After*, Edinburgh: Birlinn.

Deacon, R. (2018), 'Devolution', in B. Jones, P. Norton and O. Daddow (eds), *Politics UK*, 9th edn, London: Routledge.

Department for Constitutional Affairs (2003), *Constitutional Reform: A Supreme Court for the United Kingdom* (CP 11/03), London: The Stationery Office.

Dicey, A. V. (1959), *An Introduction to the Law of the Constitution* (first pub. 1885), 10th edn, London: Macmillan.

Dicey, A. V. (1973), *England's Case Against Home Rule* (first pub. 1886), London: Richmond Publishing Co.

Dickson, B. (2019), *Writing the United Kingdom Constitution*, Manchester: Manchester University Press.

Dorey, P. (2008), *The Labour Party and Constitutional Reform: A History of Constitutional Conservatism*, Basingstoke: Palgrave Macmillan.

Douglas-Scott, S. (2019), 'An extraordinary judgment or constitutional orthodoxy? The Supreme Court's ruling is both', *Prospect*, 24 September.

Drucker, H. M. and Brown, G. (1980), *The Politics of Nationalism and Devolution*, London: Longman.

Ekins, R. and Gee, G. (2018), '*Miller*, Constitutional Realism and the Politics of Brexit', in M. Elliott, J. Williams and A. L. Young (eds), *The UK Constitution after Miller*, Oxford: Hart Publishing.

Elliott, M. (2002), 'Parliamentary Sovereignty and the New Constitutional Order: Legislative Freedom, Political Reality and Convention', *Legal Studies*, Vol. 22, pp. 362–76.

Elliott, M. (2018), 'Sovereignty, Primacy and the Common Law Constitution: What Has EU Membership Taught Us?' in M. Elliott,

References

J. Williams and A. L. Young (eds), *The UK Constitution after Miller*, Oxford: Hart Publishing.

Elliott, M. (2019), 'The Supreme Court's judgment in Cherry/Miller (No 2): A new approach to constitutional adjudication?' *Public Law for Everyone*, 24 September. https://publiclawforeveryone.com/2019/09/24/the-supreme-courts-judgment-in-cherry-miller-no-2-a-new-approach-to-constitutional-adjudication/ accessed 3 February 2020.

Elliott, M. and Feldman, D. (2015), *Public Law*, Cambridge: Cambridge University Press.

Elliott, M., Williams, J. and Young, A. L. (2018), 'The Miller Tale: An Introduction', in M. Elliott, J. Williams and A. L. Young (eds), *The UK Constitution after Miller*, Oxford: Hart Publishing.

Evans, G. and Menon, A. (2017), *Brexit and British Politics*, Cambridge: Polity Press.

Evans, P. (ed.) (2017), *Essays on the History of Parliamentary Procedure*, Oxford: Hart Publishing.

Falconer, Lord (2006), 'The Role of Judges in a Modern Society', Magna Carta Lecture, Sydney, Australia, 13 September.

Feldman, D. (2013), 'Constitutional Conventions', in M. Qvortrup (ed.), *The British Constitution: Continuity and Change*, Oxford: Hart Publishing.

Finer, S. E. (1975), 'Adversary Politics and Electoral Reform', in S. E. Finer (ed.), *Adversary Politics and Electoral Reform*, London: Antony Wigram.

Finn, M. and Seldon, A. (2013), 'Constitutional Reform Since 1997: The Historians' Perspective', in M. Qvortrup (ed.), *The British Constitution: Continuity and Change*, Oxford: Hart Publishing.

Finnis, J. (1980), *Natural Law and Natural Rights*, Oxford: Oxford University Press.

Foley, M. (1989), *The Silence of Constitutions*, London: Routledge.

Forman, N. (1991), *Mastering British Politics*, 2nd edn, London: Macmillan.

Gallagher, J. (2016), 'Making the Case for the Union', in E. McHarg, T. Mullen, A. Page and N. Walker (eds), *The Scottish Independence Referendum*, Oxford: Oxford University Press.

Galligan, B. and Brenton, S. (2015), 'Constitutional Conventions', in B. Galligan and S. Brenton (eds), *Constitutional Conventions in Westminster Systems*, Cambridge: Cambridge University Press.

Gee, G., Hazell, R., Malleson, K. and O'Brien, P. (2015), *The Politics of Judicial Independence in the UK's Changing Constitution*, Cambridge: Cambridge University Press.

Goldsworthy, J. (1999), *The Sovereignty of Parliament: History and Philosophy*, Oxford: Clarendon Press.

Goldsworthy, J. (2010), *Parliamentary Sovereignty: Contemporary Debates*, Cambridge: Cambridge University Press.

Gordon, M. (2015), *Parliamentary Sovereignty and the UK Constitution*, Oxford: Hart Publishing.

References

Gover, D. and Kenny, M. (2018), 'Answering the West Lothian Question? A Critical Assessment of "English Votes for English Laws" in the UK Parliament', *Parliamentary Affairs*, Vol. 71 (4), pp. 760–82.

Grayling, A. C. (2017), *Democracy and its Crisis*, London: Oneworld.

Guardian (2015), 'Tax credits vote: PM accuses Lords of breaking constitutional convention', 26 October. https://www.theguardian.com/money/2015/oct/26/tax-credit-cuts-halted-as-lords-vote-to-protect-low-income-earners accessed 22 June 2020.

Guardian (2019), 'MPs back Brexit delay as votes lay bare Cabinet divisions', 14 March.

Guardian (2019), 'Parliament had failed on Brexit long before this prorogation', 29 August. https://www.theguardian.com/commentisfree/2019/aug/29/parliament-brexit-prorogue-mps-alternative-no-deal accessed 22 June 2020.

Hailsham, Lord (1976), *Elective Dictatorship*, London: BBC.

Hansard Society (2019), *Audit of Political Engagement 16: The 2019 Report*, London: Hansard Society.

Hardie, F. (1970), *The Political Influence of the British Monarchy 1867–1952*, London: Batsford.

Harris, R. (2011), *The Conservatives: A History*, London: Bantam Press.

Hart, V. (1978), *Distrust and Democracy*, Cambridge: Cambridge University Press.

Harvey, J. and Bather, L. (1963), *The British Constitution*, London: Macmillan.

Haughey, S. (2019), 'Worth Restoring? Taking Stock of the Northern Ireland Assembly', *Political Quarterly*, Vol. 70 (4), pp. 705–12.

Hayek, F. A. (1979), *Law, Liberty and Legislation, Vol. 3: The Political Order of a Free People*, London: Routledge & Kegan Paul.

Hazell, R. (ed.) (2006), *The English Question*, Manchester: Manchester University Press.

Headey, B. (1974), *British Cabinet Ministers*, London: George Allen & Unwin.

Heard, A. (1989), 'Recognizing the Variety among Constitutional Conventions', *Canadian Journal of Political Science*, Vol. 22, pp. 63–82.

Heard, A. (2012), 'Constitutional Conventions: The Heart of the Living Constitution', *Journal of Parliamentary and Political Law*, Vol. 6, pp. 319–38.

Heasman, D. J. (1967), 'The Prime Minister and the Cabinet', in W. J. Stankiewicz (ed.), *Crisis in British Government*, London: Collier-Macmillan.

Heath, G. D. (1967), 'Making the Instrument of Government', *Journal of British Studies*, Vol. 6 (2), pp. 15–34.

Henderson, A. (2019), 'Attitudes to Constitutional Change', in G. Hassan (ed.), *The Story of the Scottish Parliament*, Edinburgh: Edinburgh University Press.

Heppell, T. (2008), *Choosing the Tory Leader*, London: Tauris Academic Studies.

Heppell, T. (2010), *Choosing the Labour Leader*, London: Tauris Academic Studies.

HM Government (2010), *The Coalition: Our Programme for Government*, London: Cabinet Office.

References

Hofferbert, R. I. and Budge, I. (1992), 'The Party Mandate and the Westminster Model: Election Programmes and Government Spending in Britain, 1945–85', *British Journal of Political Science*, Vol. 22 (2), pp. 151–82.

Holland, G. (1995), 'Alas! Sir Humphrey, I Knew Him Well', *RSA Journal*, November.

Hood Phillips, O. and Jackson, P. (1978), *O. Hood Phillips' Constitutional and Administrative Law*, 6th edn, London: Sweet & Maxwell.

Horne, A. (1989), *Macmillan 1957–1986*, London: Macmillan.

House of Commons Library (2013), *The Office of Deputy Prime Minister*, SN/PC/04023, 2 July.

Howard, A. (1987), *RAB: The Life of R. A. Butler*, London: Jonathan Cape.

Howarth, D. (2017), '*Is the* Lex Parliamentaria *Really Law?*' in P. Evans (ed.), *Essays on the History of Parliamentary Procedure*, Oxford: Hart Publishing.

Howe, G. (1994), *Conflict of Loyalty*, London: Macmillan.

Hunt, M., Hooper, H. and Yowell, P. (2012), *Parliament and Human Rights: Redressing the Democratic Deficit*, Swindon: Arts and Humanities Research Council.

Independent (2019), 'Can the Queen sack Boris Johnson if he refuses to quit after MPs pass a no-confidence vote?' 10 October.

Ingham, B. (1991), *Kill the Messenger*, London: HarperCollins.

Jaconelli, J. (2013), 'Continuity and Change in Constitutional Conventions', in M. Qvortrup (ed.), *The British Constitution: Continuity and Change*, Oxford: Hart Publishing.

Jefferson, K. W. (2011), *Celtic Politics*, Lanham: University Press of America.

Jeffery, C., Henderson, A., Scully, R. and Wyn Jones, R. (2016), 'England's Dissatisfactions and the Conservative Dilemma', *Political Studies Review*, Vol. 14 (3), pp. 335–48.

Jennings, I. (1959), *The Law and the Constitution*, 5th edn, London: University of London Press.

Jensen, C. S. (2003), 'Neo-Functionalism', in M. Cini (ed.), *European Union Politics*, Oxford: Oxford University Press.

Joint Committee on Conventions (2006), *Conventions of the UK Constitution*, First Report, Session 2005–06, HL Paper 265-I, HC 1212-I, London: The Stationery Office.

Joint Committee on Parliamentary Privilege (1999), *Report*, Session 1998–99, HC 214-I, HL Paper 43-I, London: The Stationery Office.

Justice Committee, House of Commons (2009), *Devolution: A Decade On*, Vol. 1, Fifth Report, Session 2008–09, HC 529-I, London: The Stationery Office.

Kaiser, A. (2008), 'Parliamentary Opposition in Westminster Democracies: Britain, Canada, Australia and New Zealand', *The Journal of Legislative Studies*, Vol. 14 (1/2), pp. 20–45.

Keith, A. B. (1952), *The British Cabinet System*, 2nd edn by N. H. Gibbs, London: Stevens & Sons.

References

Keir, D. L. (1966), *The Constitutional History of Modern Britain since 1485*, 8th edn, London: Black.

Kenealy, D., Eichhorn, J., Parry, R., Paterson, L. and Remold, A. (2017), *Publics, Elites and Constitutional Change in the UK: A Missed Opportunity?* Basingstoke: Palgrave Macmillan.

King, A. (1976), 'Modes of Executive-Legislative Relations: Great Britain, France, and West Germany', *Legislative Studies Quarterly*, Vol. 1 (1), pp. 11–34.

King, A. (1977), *Britain Says Yes*, Washington, DC: American Enterprise Institute.

King, A. (2007), *The British Constitution*, Oxford: Oxford University Press.

King, J. (2019), 'The Democratic Case for a Written Constitution', *Current Legal Problems*, Vol. 72 (1), pp. 1–36.

Kitzinger, U. (1973), *Diplomacy and Persuasion*, London: Thames & Hudson.

LeDuc, L., Niemi, R. G. and Norris, P. (eds) (2010), *Comparing Democracies 3: Elections and Voting in the 21st Century*, London: Sage.

LeMay, G. H. (1979), *The Victorian Constitution*, London: Duckworth.

Le Sueur, A. and Simson Caird, J. (2013), 'The House of Lords Select Committee on the Constitution', in A. Horne, G. Drewry and D. Oliver (eds), *Parliament and the Law*, Oxford: Hart Publishing.

Le Sueur, A., Sunkin, M. and Murkens, J. E. H. (2016), *Public Law: Texts, Cases and Materials*, 3rd edn, Oxford: Oxford University Press.

Leyland, P. (2016), *The Constitution of the United Kingdom: A Contextual Analysis*, London: Bloomsbury.

Lijphart, A. (1984), *Democracies*, New Haven: Yale University Press.

McConalogue, J. (2020), *The British Constitution Resettled*, Cham: Palgrave Macmillan.

McEwen, N. (2016), 'A Constitution in Flux', in E. McHarg, T. Mullen, A. Page and N. Walker (eds), *The Scottish Independence Referendum*, Oxford: Oxford University Press.

McHarg, A. (2016), 'The Constitutional Case for Independence', in E. McHarg, T. Mullen, A. Page and N. Walker (eds), *The Scottish Independence Referendum*, Oxford: Oxford University Press.

Mackenzie, K. (1968), *The English Parliament*, revised edn, Harmondsworth: Penguin Books.

Markesinis, B. S. (1972), *The Theory and Practice of Dissolution of Parliament*, Cambridge: Cambridge University Press.

Marshall, G. (1967), 'Parliament and the Constitution', in W. J. Stankiewicz (ed.), *Crisis in British Government*, London: Collier-Macmillan.

Marshall, G. (1984), *Constitutional Conventions*, Oxford: Clarendon Press.

Marshall, G. and Moodie, G. C. (1967), *Some Problems of the Constitution*, 4th revised edn, London: Hutchinson University Library.

Maxwell, P. (1999), 'The House of Lords as a Constitutional Court: The Implications of *Ex Parte EOC*', in B. Dickson and P. Carmichael (eds),

References

The House of Lords: Its Parliamentary and Judicial Roles, Oxford: Hart Publishing.

Mill, J. S. (1968), *Considerations on Representative Government* (first pub. 1861), London: Everyman Library.

Morton, P. (1991–2), 'Conventions of the British Constitution', *Holdsworth Law Review*, Vol. 15, pp. 114–80.

Nagle, J. (2018), 'Between Conflict and Peace: An Analysis of the Complex Consequences of the Good Friday Agreement', *Parliamentary Affairs*, Vol. 71 (2), pp. 395–416.

Natzler, D. (ed.) (2019), *Erskine May's Treatise on The Law, Privileges, Proceedings and Usage of Parliament*, 25th edn, London: LexisNexis.

Nicolson, H. (1952), *King George The Fifth: His Life and Reign*, London: Constable & Co.

Norton, P. (1975), *Dissension in the House of Commons 1945–1974*, London: Macmillan.

Norton, P. (1978a), 'Government Defeats in the House of Commons: Myth and Reality', *Public Law*, Winter, pp. 360–78.

Norton, P. (1978b), *Conservative Dissidents*, London: Temple Smith.

Norton, P. (1981), *The Commons in Perspective*, Oxford: Martin Robertson.

Norton, P. (1982), *The Constitution in Flux*, Oxford: Martin Robertson.

Norton, P. (1989), 'Collective Ministerial Responsibility', *Social Studies Review*, Vol. 5 (1), pp. 33–6.

Norton, P. (1996a), 'The United Kingdom: Political Conflict, Parliamentary Scrutiny', in P. Norton (ed.), *National Parliaments and the European Union*, London: Frank Cass.

Norton, P. (1996b), 'The Party Leader', in P. Norton (ed.), *The Conservative Party*, London: Prentice Hall/Harvester Wheatsheaf.

Norton, P. (1996c), 'Conservative Politics and the Abolition of Stormont', in P. Catterall and S. McDougall (eds), *The Northern Ireland Question in British Politics*, Basingstoke: Palgrave Macmillan.

Norton, P. (1998), 'The Conservative Party: "In Office but Not in Power"', in A. King (ed.), *New Labour Triumphs: Britain at the Polls*, Chatham: Chatham House Publishers.

Norton, P. (2000), 'Would Fixed-Term Parliaments Enhance Democracy?' in L. Robins and B. Jones (eds), *Debates in British Politics Today*, Manchester: Manchester University Press.

Norton, P. (2001), 'Playing by the Rules: The Constraining Hand of Parliamentary Procedure', *The Journal of Legislative Studies*, Vol. 7 (3), pp. 13–33.

Norton, P. (2005), 'Parliament and the Courts', in N. D. J. Baldwin (ed.), *Parliament in the 21st Century*, London: Politico's.

Norton, P. (2006), 'The Constitution: Selective Incrementalism Continues', in M. Rush and P. Giddings (eds), *The Palgrave Review of British Politics 2005*, Basingstoke: Palgrave Macmillan.

References

Norton, P. (2007), 'The Constitution: Fragmentation or Adaptation?', in M. Rush and P. Giddings (eds), *The Palgrave Review of British Politics 2006*, Basingstoke: Palgrave Macmillan.

Norton, P. (2010), *The British Polity*, 5th edn, Boston: Longman.

Norton, P. (2011a), 'Introduction: A Century of Change', *Parliamentary History*, Vol. 30 (1), pp. 1–18.

Norton, P. (2011b), 'The Englishness of Westminster', in A. Aughey and C. Berberich (eds), *These Englands*, Manchester: Manchester University Press.

Norton, P. (2012a), 'Constitutional Change and the Tensions of Liberal Democracy', in J. Connelly and J. Hayward (eds), *The Withering of the Welfare State: Regression*, Basingstoke: Palgrave Macmillan.

Norton, P. (2012b), 'Speaking for the People: A Conservative Narrative of Democracy', *Policy Studies*, Vol. 33 (2), pp. 121–32.

Norton, P. (2012c), 'Resisting the Inevitable? The Parliament Act 1911', *Parliamentary History*, Vol. 31 (3), pp. 444–59.

Norton, P. (2012d), 'Opt-Out: Britain's Unsplendid Isolation', in J. Hayward and R. Wurzel (eds), *European Disunion: Between Sovereignty and Solidarity*, Basingstoke: Palgrave Macmillan.

Norton, P. (2013a), 'A Democratic Dialogue? Parliament and Human Rights in the United Kingdom', *Asia Pacific Law Review*, Vol. 21 (2), pp. 141–66.

Norton, P. (2013b), 'Maintaining the Balance? The Relationship of Parliaments to Other Branches of Government', in M. Diamant, M. L. Van Emmerik, J. P. Loof and W. J. M. Voermans (eds), *The Powers That Be*, Oisterwijk: Wolf Legal Publishers.

Norton, P. (2013c), *Parliament in British Politics*, 2nd edn, Basingstoke: Palgrave Macmillan.

Norton, P. (2013d), 'Parliament Act 1911 in its Historical Context', in D. Feldman (ed.), *Law in Politics, Politics in Law*, Oxford: Hart Publishing.

Norton, P. (2013e), *The Voice of the Backbenchers. The 1922: The First 90 Years, 1923–2013*, London: Conservative History Group.

Norton, P. (2014), 'From Flexible to Semi-Fixed: The Fixed-Term Parliaments Act', *Journal of Comparative and International Law (JICL)*, Vol. 1 (2), pp. 203–20.

Norton, P. (2015a), 'Parliament and the Courts: Strangers, Foes or Friends?' *The UK Supreme Court Yearbook 2015*, Vol. 6: Legal Year 2014–15, Cambridge: Appellate Press.

Norton, P. (2015b), 'The Coalition and the Conservatives', in A. Seldon and M. Finn (eds), *The Coalition Effect 2010–2015*, Cambridge: Cambridge University Press.

Norton, P. (2016a), *The Continuing Relevance of Magna Carta: Symbol or Substance?* Hull: University of Hull.

Norton, P. (2016b), 'The Fixed-Term Parliaments Act and Votes of Confidence', *Parliamentary Affairs*, Vol. 69 (1), pp. 3–18.

References

Norton, P. (2016c), 'A Temporary Occupant of No. 10? Prime Ministerial Succession in the Event of the Death of the Incumbent', *Public Law*, January, pp. 18–34.

Norton, P. (2017a), 'The Constitution', in K. Hickson and B. Williams (eds), *John Major: An Unsuccessful Prime Minister? Reappraising John Major*, London: Biteback.

Norton, P. (2017b). *Reform of the House of Lords*, Manchester: Manchester University Press.

Norton, P. (2017c), 'Legislatures and the Courts: The Importance of Place', *Journal of International and Comparative Law*, Vol. 4 (2), pp. 171–88.

Norton, P. (2018a), 'The Judiciary', in B. Jones, P. Norton and O. Daddow (eds), *Politics UK*, 9th edn, London: Routledge.

Norton, P. (2018b), 'Ministers, Departments and Civil Servants', in B. Jones, P. Norton and O. Daddow (eds), *Politics UK*, 9th edn, London: Routledge.

Norton, P. (2019a), 'Is the House of Commons Too Powerful? The 2019 Bingham Lecture in Constitutional Studies, University of Oxford', *Parliamentary Affairs*, Vol. 72 (4), pp. 996–1013.

Norton, P. (2019b), 'Power Behind the Scenes: The Importance of Informal Space in Legislatures', *Parliamentary Affairs*, Vol. 72 (2), pp. 245–66.

Norton, P. and Maer, L. (2018), 'Relationship between the Two Houses', in A. Horne and G. Drewry (eds), *Parliament and the Law*, 2nd edn, Oxford: Hart Publishing.

O'Leary, B. and McGarry, J. (eds) (1990), *The Future of Northern Ireland*, Oxford: Clarendon Press.

Political and Constitutional Reform Committee, House of Commons (2010), *Fixed-Term Parliaments Bill*, Second Report, Session 2010–12, HC 436, London: The Stationery Office.

Political and Constitutional Reform Committee, House of Commons (2013), *The Role and Powers of the Prime Minister: The Impact of the Fixed-Term Parliaments Act 2011 on Government*, Fourth Report, Session 2013–14, HC 440, London: The Stationery Office.

PoliticsHome (2019), 'After this Brexit madness, will things ever be the same again?', 13 March. https://www.politicshome.com/news/article/after-this-brexit-madness-will-things-ever-be-the-same-again accessed 25 March 2020.

Pollard, A. F. (1920), *The Evolution of Parliament*, London: Longman, Green & Co.

Public Administration and Constitutional Affairs Committee, House of Commons (2016), *The Strathclyde Review: Statutory Instruments and the Power of the House of Lords*, Eighth Report, Session 2015–16, HC 752, London: The Stationery Office.

Public Administration Committee, House of Commons (2004), *Taming the Prerogative: Strengthening Ministerial Accountability to Parliament*, Fourth Report, Session 2003–4, HC 422, London: The Stationery Office.

References

Public Administration Committee, House of Commons (2013), *Truth to Power: How Civil Service Reform Can Succeed*, Eighth Report, Session 2013–14, HC 74, London: The Stationery Office.

Qvortrup, M. (2005), *A Comparative Study of Referendums*, 2nd edn, Manchester: Manchester University Press.

Qvortrup, M. (2018a), *Referendums Around the World*, Basingstoke: Palgrave Macmillan.

Qvortrup, M. (2018b), *Government by Referendum*, Manchester: Manchester University Press.

Redlich, J. (1908), *The Procedure of the House of Commons: A Study of its History and Present Form*, Vol. 1, London: Archibald Constable.

Richards, P. G. (1984), *Mackintosh's The Government and Politics of Britain*, 6th edn, London: Hutchinson.

Roberts, A. (2014), *The Holy Fox: The Life of Lord Halifax*, London: Head of Zeus.

Rose, R. (1984), *Do Parties Make a Difference?* 2nd edn, London: Macmillan, 1984.

Royal Commission on the Constitution (1973), *Report*, Vol. 1, Cmnd. 5460, London: HMSO.

Sampson, E. (2017), 'Privilege: The Unfolding Debate with the Courts', in P. Evans (ed.), *Essays on the History of Parliamentary Procedure*, Oxford: Hart Publishing.

Sedgemore, B. (1980), *The Secret Constitution*, London: Hodder & Stoughton.

Seldon, A. (1997), *Major: A Political Life*, London: Weidenfeld & Nicolson.

Seldon, A. (2019), *May at 10*, London: Biteback Publishing.

Select Committee on the Barnett Formula (2009), *The Barnett Formula*, 1st Report, Session 2008–09, HL Paper 139, London: The Stationery Office.

Shirlow, P. (2018), 'Twenty Years after the Belfast Agreement', *Parliamentary Affairs*, Vol. 71 (2), pp. 392–4.

Simcock, A. J. C. (1992), 'One and Many: The Office of Secretary of State', *Public Administration*, Vol. 70 (4), pp. 535–53.

Stevens, R. (2002), *The English Judges*, Oxford: Hart Publishing.

Strathclyde Review (2015), *Strathclyde Review: Secondary Legislation and the Primacy of the House of Commons*, Cm 9177, London: The Cabinet Office.

Straw, J. (2012), *Last Man Standing*, London: Macmillan.

Strong, J. (2014), 'Why Parliament Now Decides on War: Tracing the Growth of the Parliamentary Prerogative through Syria, Libya and Iraq', *The British Journal of Politics and International Relations*, Vol. 17 (4), pp. 19–34.

Sumption, J. (2015), 'Magna Carta Then and Now', Address to the Friends of the British Library, 9 March.

Sunstein, C. (2001), *Designing Democracy; What Constitutions Do*, Oxford: Oxford University Press.

Taylor, S. (1998), 'Robert Walpole, First Earl of Orford', in R. Eccleshall and G. Walker (eds), *Biographical Dictionary of British Prime Ministers*, London: Routledge.

References

Teague, P. (2019), 'Brexit, the Belfast Agreement and Northern Ireland: Imperilling a Fragile Political Bargain', *Political Quarterly*, Vol. 90 (4), pp. 690–704.

Thatcher, M. (1988), *Britain and Europe*, London: Conservative Political Centre.

Thimont Jack, M., Owen, J., Paun, A. and Kellam, J. (2018), *Devolution after Brexit*, London: Institute for Government.

Thomas of Cwmgiedd, Lord (2014), 'The Judiciary, the Executive and Parliament: Relationships and the Rule of Law', Address to the Institute for Government, 1 December.

Thomas of Cwmgiedd, Lord (2017), 'The Judiciary within the State: The Relationship between the Branches of the State', Michael Ryle Memorial Lecture, 15 June.

Thornton, S. and Kirkup, J. (2017), 'Was Damian Green really called Deputy Prime Minister?' *LSE Blog*, 22 December, http://blogs.lse.ac.uk/politicsandpolicy/62576–2/ accessed 30 December 2017.

Thorpe, D. R. (2010), *Supermac: The Life of Harold Macmillan*, London: Chatto & Windus.

The Times (1950), 'Letters', 2 May.

The Times (2005), 'Boundaries between judges and Parliament will be battleground', 16 September.

The Times (2019), '"Sack me if you dare" Boris Johnson will tell the Queen', 6 October.

Todd, J. (2005), 'A New Territorial Politics in the British Isles?' in J. Coakley, B. Laffan and J. Todd (eds), *Renovation or Revolution? New Territorial Politics in Ireland and the United Kingdom*, Dublin: University College Dublin Press.

Tompkins, A. (2003), *Public Law*, Oxford: Oxford University Press.

Turpin, C. (1985), 'Ministerial Responsibility: Myth or Reality?' in J. Jowell and D. Oliver (eds), *The Changing Constitution*, Oxford: Oxford University Press.

Wheare, K. (1951), *Modern Constitutions*, Oxford: Oxford University Press.

Wheeler-Bennett, J. (1958), *George VI: His Life and Reign*, London: Macmillan.

White, J. V. (2009), 'The Judicial Office', in L. Blom-Cooper, B. Dickson and G. Drewry (eds), *The Judicial House of Lords 1876–2009*, Oxford: Oxford University Press.

Wilson, H. (1971), *A Personal Record: The Labour Government 1964–1970*, Boston: Little, Brown & Co.

Wilson, H. (1977), *The Governance of Britain*, London: Sphere Books.

Young, A. (2009), *Parliamentary Sovereignty and the Human Rights Act*, Oxford: Hart Publishing.

Young, A. (2017), *Democratic Dialogue and the Constitution*, Oxford: Oxford University Press.

Index

Index

Index

Index

Index

'backstop' 61, 179
Northern Ireland Act 1998 81, 176
Northern Ireland Assembly 176–7
Northern Ireland (Executive
Formation and Exercise of
Functions) Act 2019 177

O'Leary, B. 174
opposition, the 5, 37, 51, 107–8, 121,
123, 129
Leader of 42, 61, 121, 124, 131, 137
Osborne, George 145
Owen, Lord 79

Padfield case 90
Palmerston, Lord 133, 161
parliament 4–6, 9, 14, 18, 22–9,
34–5, 38–9, 44, 47–8, 51, 53, 65,
67–72, 75–8, 80–1, 83–5, 89–95,
97–8, 100–7, 111, 113, 115–18,
120, 122, 124–6, 129–30, 154–7,
162, 165, 167, 177, 180
see also House of Commons;
House of Lords
Parliament Act 1911 26–7, 42, 68,
115, 126
Parliament Act 1949 26–7
Parliamentary Oaths Act 1866 109
Parliamentary Papers Act 1840 105
parliamentary privilege 95,
100–5, 111
Committees on 103–5, 112–13
parliamentary sovereignty 4–5, 7,
18–19, 22–30, 75, 77–8, 81, 83,
95, 97, 167, 176, 180
Parliament Square 86–7
PC *see* Plaid Cymru
Peel, Sir Robert 135
Peerages Act 1963 38
Pepper v Hart 106
Phillips of Worth Matravers, Lord
96, 102
Pickthorn, Sir Kenneth 106, 148, 150

Pitt, William 161
Plaid Cymru (PC) 169
Political and Constitutional
Reform Committee, House of
Commons 119, 123
Political Parties, Elections and
Referendums Bill 79
Ponsonby, Arthur 44
Ponsonby Rule 44–5
Popper, Karl 7
Portillo, Michael 136
Powell, Charles 143
Powell, Enoch 52
Prescott, John 143–5, 149–50
President of the Supreme Court 92
prime minister 9, 33, 35–41, 43,
46–8, 58, 60, 63, 72, 74, 84–5,
96–7, 116, 120–2, 124–6,
128–45, 147, 149–52, 160–5
deputy 116–17, 141–52, 163
Prior, Jim 162
prisoner voting 21, 85–6
prorogation 48, 63, 65, 84, 97,
104, 124–5
Public Administration Committee,
House of Commons 44, 156

R. v Secretary of State for Employment
[*EOC* case] 55
Raab, Dominic 145
Redlich, Josef 107
Rees-Mogg, Jacob 44
Rees-Mogg, Lord 57
referendums 9, 10–11, 15, 51, 58–9,
67–81, 111, 163, 169–71, 173,
175, 178
Reform Acts 5
(1867) 38
Reform Bill 161
respective autonomy model 83–4,
89–92, 98
Restoration (1660) 4
Richards, Peter 155–6

201

Index

Index